The Believer's Edge

It's my pleasure to send you this complimentary copy of my new book. In doing so I am hopeful of three things.

First, I hope you enjoy it. It's a brief parable that illustrates the benefits of religious faith and practice. Scientific research reveals that religiously active people make good neighbors, build better communities and live happier, healthier lives. But scientific studies are dull. So I wrote *The Believer's Edge* to present the fruits of that research in a charming parable.

Second, I hope you recommend it to others. If they are active in a faith-based community, they will find it affirming. If they aren't active, perhaps this book will help them in the same way that Derek is helped in the parable.

Finally, if opportunities arise, I hope you will recommend me as a speaker or help arrange a book signing for a church, school, club or other faith-based organization. I'd like to see revenues from the sale of this book help underwrite the good work of church people — especially young people — in local communities.

If any of this raises any questions in your mind, please contact me in the way you find most convenient.

> Email: ophelps@MidwestLeadershipInstitute.net
> Phone: 815-248-2977
> 208 E. North St., Durand, IL 61024

May God continue to bless you and all whom you love,

Sample speaking topics:
- Parents: Hang in There! *Your kids deserve it — even if they don't like it*
- Seeing Is Believing! *What research says about the benefits of being active in a faith communty*
- Church-goers Make Better Lovers! *And a lot of other good things*
- Don't Be Caught Dead in Church: Let Your Light Shine!
- Going to Church Makes Good Sense for Saints — And Even Better Sense for Sinners!

THE BELIEVER'S EDGE

The secret to a healthier, happier, more significant life

Owen Phelps, Ph.D.

For Bill & Vicki ~ With deep fondness & appreciation for two wonderful co-workers in the vineyard ~ Cherish the Edge always! 11/05

TDC
The Durand Corporation
Durand, Illinois 61024

THE BELIEVER'S EDGE

The Midwest Leadership Institute (MLI) is a wholly-owned subsidiary of The Durand Corporation (TDC). For more information about this book, its author, TDC or MLI, visit MLI's World Wide Web site:
http://www.MidwestLeadershipInstitute.net

Library of Congress Control Number: 2005907591

ISBN 0-9769210-0-6

Printed in the United States of America.

To order additional copies, contact:

The Durand Corporation
208 E. North St.
Durand, IL 61024

Here4U@MidwestLeadershipInstitute.net
http://www.MidwestLeadershipInstitute.net

Dedication

To my mother, wife and children, who have
helped keep me connected to a Christian
community for so many years.

TABLE OF CONTENTS

Introduction:

ACTIVE BELIEVERS MAKE GOOD NEIGHBORS

In 2001, three dozen community foundations and other organizations released the results of the *Social Capital Community Benchmark Survey* — the largest survey ever conducted on the civic engagement of Americans.

The purpose of this study of nearly 30,000 people was to lay "the groundwork for a multi-year effort to rebuild community bonds."

The survey discovered that the people most likely to be involved in working for the good of their communities are active in religious organizations. They're also the people who are generally most tolerant of cultural diversity in our communities.

Surprised?

You are if you believe two common criticisms related to religion today. First, there's the view that religion is primarily a divisive force in human affairs. Second, there's the view that members of religious organizations are intolerant of others. If you're inclined to accept either of these criticisms, consider these findings from the survey:

■ "Involvement in religious communities is among the strongest predictors of giving and volunteering both for religious and secular causes."

■ "Religious people ... are great at doing (things) for (others)."

- "Religious involvement is positively associated with most other forms of civic involvement."
- "Religiously engaged people are more likely than religiously disengaged people to be involved in civic groups of all sorts, to vote, to be active in community affairs, to give blood, to trust other people (from shopkeepers to neighbors), to know the names of public officials, to socialize with friends and neighbors, and even simply to have a wider circle of friends."

In short, the study found that *communities benefit* in many ways when their citizens are actively engaged in the practice of their faiths.

Not only do our villages, towns and cities benefit from people who are religiously active. Other studies suggest that *people themselves benefit* from their active association with religious organizations.

In a phrase, active believers seem to lead healthier and happier lives.

The *Social Capital Community Benchmark Survey* also reported something other studies have found: there is a big disconnect in America between *having faith* and *practicing faith*.

The survey found, for example, that 84% of the people questioned agreed that religion was very important to them. But only 58% were members of a local church and just 45% reported they engaged in religious activities about once a week or more.

A Gallup poll conducted in December 1999 reported similar results: 86% of those responding said they believed in God and another 8% said they believed in some kind of "universal spirit or higher power" — meaning that 94% of those surveyed were, in the broad sense, *believers.* Yet only 54% said they were *religious.*

Why this disconnect between belief and practice?

There is no one simple reason. People are complex, and so are their motivations — both for doing things and not doing them.

Social scientists have offered a number of possible reasons why so many people don't integrate their beliefs and actions, and these scientists continue to search for even more definitive reasons. What they are learning can be fascinating.

This book has a more humble purpose. It does not explore why so many millions of believers shun religious affiliation and practice. It exists only to remind people — with a simple parable — of the real, practical and empirically verified benefits of belonging to and being active in a religious organization.

If you're looking for a way to lead a happier, healthier and more meaningful life — *or if you want to help someone else find a way to do that* — this little book could be the key to unlocking that opportunity.

Why not read on and see for yourself?

RENEWING ACQUAINTANCES

Derek looked up at the lights over the elevator door and watched them climb toward Tom's floor. It was early, long before the morning rush, and he was alone. But he knew Tom was an early riser, and he wanted some time with Tom alone before the pace picked up and Tom's day would begin to fill up with distractions.

They had known each other for a long time, going way back to high school. They had gone their separate ways to college. Then both returned to town and took jobs with the same firm. But they weren't really all that close.

Derek was an outgoing type — part of the popular crowd in high school. He played football, dated a cheerleader, "the whole thing," as they said back then. In college he didn't play interscholastic sports, but he joined a fraternity and had a good time. He managed to learn a bit while posting average grades before he eventually walked across the stage, picked up his diploma, accepted congratulations from his parents and headed off to another party.

Derek was hoping to be offered a job in a big city several hours away, where a lot of his friends were from and where most of them were returning after graduation. But the only solid offer he got was a sales position with his hometown's biggest employer and the money looked good. His frat buddies assured him that he could sell refrigerators to Eskimos. But what cinched it for him was the girl who greeted him at the door when he went to interview for the job. She was incredibly gorgeous and friendly too. He had already lined up a date with her when the interviewer called him in and offered him the job. "What's not to like?" he concluded as he accepted the offer on the spot. He couldn't wait to get out of that office and renew the quickly budding romance that had just ignited out in the reception area.

Tom had it harder. He was the first of his family to attend college and he had to work his way through. Once money was so tight he had to drop out for a semester and work two jobs to get caught up on his bills. That made getting his degree all the more important to him. Fortunately, his studies came easy to him and he enjoyed the opportunity to spend time with his professors. His favorite past-time was reading. He was only half-joking when he told his mother that he had become an obsessive reader because the college had a huge library and its treasures came free with tuition. "Free" was a critical consideration as he struggled to cover the cost of his schooling.

When he graduated Tom was grateful to be offered a job by a hometown firm because it allowed him to stay with his folks and keep expenses down. His dad co-signed for a loan that let him purchase a used car and some new clothes to wear for work.

That was 15 years ago. In those years Tom and Derek had not seen much of each other, except at company social functions. Derek was in sales and traveled about half the week. Eventually he had married that gorgeous receptionist, moved to the fashionable north end of town, and together they had two children. Tom was in accounting and it seemed like he never left his office. Derek always saw him there when he rode up on the elevator to drop off his monthly expense report. If he caught Tom's eye, he'd always wave. Once or twice a year he'd stop in to share some news about one of their old classmates. But that was about it. As Derek explained to his wife once after one of the company social events, "Sure, Tom's a real nice guy, but we just don't seem to have much in common."

At the same time, Derek had to admit — at least to himself — that he respected Tom, even though he wasn't quite sure why.

Derek pondered that as the elevator moved up towards the accounting floor. Maybe it was because Tom was so bright. That was part of it. But there seemed to be more, and Derek couldn't put his finger on it. Maybe it was, as his dad liked to say about dependable people, "he always seems to have both oars in the water." Tom was steady. Stable. He just seemed "to have his head screwed on right."

Anyway, it didn't really matter. Derek didn't know where else to turn. He needed to talk with someone — quickly. He wasn't comfortable with his situation. He wasn't used to needing help from anyone. But he needed it now, and what else are old friends for? Tom always seemed to have a good handle on things. Why not give him a try?

MIDLIFE MALAISE

The elevator's bell bought him back to the present. He stepped off and reassured himself that the receptionist was not yet on duty. He looked across her desk and saw Tom looking up. He must have heard the bell or been distracted by the elevator's doors opening at this early hour. Derek waved. "Hey Tom, got a minute?" Derek asked as he walked toward the door to Tom's office. Tom stood, stepped around his desk, extended his hand in a sweeping gesture, then shook Derek's hand firmly, offered a big smile and said, "Sure, what can I do for you?"

Derek was put at ease. He wasn't sure how to start. But he was glad Tom hadn't commented on the early hour or the empty building or how in 15 years Derek had never approached him this way. Tom made it seem that this meeting was ordinary. Derek was encouraged by that. But he wasn't relaxed. Not at all. He started with a little small talk, the kind of thing he was so good at when he had to break the ice on a cold call. They didn't call him "The Master" for nothing. Derek could warm up a whole room of grouchy skeptics in under a minute. He had been doing it all his life, and he made a very good living at it — if you kept life's score by counting money.

"How's the bride? How are the kids? Your folks doing okay?" Derek kept up the questions for a few minutes while Tom responded positively but without elaborating. Pretty soon Derek's bag of quick, easy, superficial questions was empty. He tried to keep things moving — and distant — with an open-ended question about the affliction one of their classmates had come down with. But Tom deflected it pretty quickly, saying: "It's a cross he's going to bear for as long as he lives." After that the room was silent for what seemed to Derek like an eternity. Probably no more than 10 seconds had passed when Tom took pity on Derek and broke the ice. "What brings you by?" he asked, his tone still casual.

Derek looked up and into Tom's eyes. "You sure you don't mind?" he asked, secretly desperate for a little reassurance. Tom sensed his unease. "We've known each other for a long time, Derek. What's on your mind?" Tom's tone indicated he was interested — and interested in helping. But not *too* interested. That was good. Derek didn't want to feel like a specimen under a microscope. He was uncomfortable enough without Tom starting to pry.

"Tom," Derek said, more softly than Tom had ever heard him speak before, "this isn't easy for me." Tom looked Derek in the eye. "Go ahead," he said just as softly. After a few seconds, Derek took a deep breath and put the issue on the table. "Sally and I are having trouble, Tom." There was a pause. But before Tom could say anything, Derek added. "I really don't know what to do about it." Tom let a little quiet pass before he said, very softly and slowly, "What's happening, Derek?" He kept the question as general and open-ended as he could. He wanted to encourage Derek to say more, and he knew if it appeared that he was prying, Derek would close up and be out the door.

"That's the problem, Tom," Derek said. His tone was louder and more urgent. "I don't really know what the trouble is. If I did, I could do something about it. But I just can't get a handle on it. And Tom, it's not just about Sally. It's about work here too. Things just aren't going well. It's like I'm driving down a road and the whole surface is covered with rumble strips. Everything's bumpy. All the time. And I just can't get a handle on it."

Tom didn't respond right away. He kept looking into Derek's eyes as he let a little smile — a little *sympathetic* smile, he hoped — creep across his face. If Derek wanted to say more, Tom didn't want to interject. But if Derek needed more encouragement, Tom wanted to provide it. In a moment, it was clear that Derek needed a little more encouragement. "Are you confused? Is that what's bothering you?" Tom asked. He knew that wasn't the problem — at least not the deeper problem — but he didn't want to probe too deeply. He feared that could prompt Derek to pull back.

"Confused? Yeah, I'm confused all right," Derek said with a bit of a chuckle. "But that's not really the problem. It's something else — and the problem is, I'm not sure what." He looked down to the floor. After a few seconds of silence, Tom decided it was safe to try to move the process along just a bit. "Why don't you just talk about it and see what surfaces?" he asked softly.

"Well, it's not what you think?" Derek said.

"And what do I think?" Tom asked, his smile growing. He thought it appropriate to lighten the mood just a bit.

Derek was quick to reply: "I mean, it's not that I'm cheating on Sally or anything like that. I don't have a mistress. I don't hit her. I don't abuse the kids either. But there's no joy in our house. I don't know what's going through Sally's mind. And I don't have a clue about what the kids are thinking — except I'm pretty sure it's never about me. Near as I can tell, they might not even notice if I went out the door some morning and never came back — unless, maybe, the money ran out and they couldn't have everything they want. Our whole life just feels so empty and uncaring. We have everything and we appreciate nothing. It's like that author we read in school — what's his name? — Thoreau said, I feel like I'm leading a life of *quiet desperation.* I think we all are, Sally and the kids too. When you scratch below the surface, we're all pretty miserable, and I feel helpless to do anything about it. I'd like to be part of the solution, but it's obvious to me I'm part of the problem. You know what I mean?" he asked, obviously looking for assurance.

"Yeah," Tom said in a resigned tone, nodding his head and managing a small smile. "I think I know what you mean."

Tom had married Michelle, a girl his younger sister had introduced him to not long after he had graduated from college, while he was still living at home trying to keep expenses down. They dated for about a year and a half before he popped the question. "What have you been waiting for?" she replied. "Yes or no?" he persisted, so nervous he didn't get her drift. "Well yes, of course I will," she said. "But what have you been waiting for? I thought you'd never ask."

He was sure he wanted to marry her only a month or two after they started dating, and in the ensuing months they had even talked about what names they would give their children, how many they wanted to have, and what kind of a house they would all live in. For some reason, Michelle had her eye on a tri-level back then. Tom didn't care. But he wanted a basketball goal in the driveway. "And not just for the boys," he told her. *"Boys?"* she had teased. "You want more than one?"

Tom was not a gifted athlete and he had never played interscholastic sports. But he enjoyed intramural sports. At least he wasn't the kid who was always picked last, although he had worried about it a couple of times. Most of all, he had fond memories of playing hoops with his dad when he was young. His dad taught him the fundamentals without making it a chore, so Tom never embarrassed himself even though he was never the tallest or fastest kid on the block. He appreciated that and realized that his dad had done a lot for him.

He told Michelle he wanted to be as good a father to their children as his own dad had been to him. They were in the car, sitting outside her home, and she was admiring the diamond he had been saving so long to buy. She had looked up into his eyes, smiled a smile that was nearly beatific, took his cheeks in her hands and drew him close, giving him a big, deep kiss. "I'm sure you will," she said. "And I'll try to be as good a mother as my mom has been to me," she added. "You will," he assured her, just before he kissed her back.

The years had been pretty good to them. They had been married 12 years and they had four children — two boys and two girls. When the weather was good, it was not strange to see the whole crew out in the driveway playing a game of family basketball. The big ones had to learn how to take it easy with the little ones around. That didn't always go too smoothly, and even when it did, there were little accidents. Little scratches and bumps. But mom and dad were always ready with a quick hug and a kiss. And the big kids, if they were inadvertently at fault, really poured on the syrup with the little ones. Often as not, once the tears stopped, the moment ended with tickles and snuggles and laughs — and the little one in the ordeal finally declaring, "Now I'm *really* going to get you." Invariably, then, the big one let the little one shine.

Tom felt blessed. But he also had to admit that some of the best "Kodak moments" were already lost forever. He noticed that even the youngest children didn't come running to greet him, their arms out wide, their voices and faces bursting with joy, as they had in those first couple of years after they learned to walk. Now when he walked in after work and announced with a flourish, "I'm home," one or two of the kids might say, "Hi, Dad." But just as often they would not even acknowledge his greeting. And sometimes no one was home. The oldest, a girl, was on a school team and had to be picked up from practice. The second oldest, a boy, was in club sports. Both of them took piano lessons. The youngest ones were getting involved in things too, and sometimes Tom felt like none of them had time for him anymore at all.

Michelle seemed to have even less time! Fortunately they could joke about it. "Remember how we got married and stopped seeing each other?" Tom would ask her. "What year was that?"

"It was the year you said you wanted boys and girls — not a boy *or* girl, or a boy *and* a girl — but *boys and girls.* Remember, sweetie?" Michelle would reply.

"Sure, I remember," Tom would tease and retort, "Wasn't it the same year you said you'd like to have 15 kids?"

"I still do," Michelle once declared, to Tom's amazement. Then she smiled: "But with a kid like you around, I just don't have the time."

They cherished their little time together, and they tried hard not to resent its scarcity now that the house was full of children. They both agreed that the children were a real blessing, worth infinitely more than the sacrifices they required. Tom and Michelle also both made time to do things with the kids, knowing their time to share each stage of development with each child was incredibly fleeting.

Through it all they tried very hard to set time aside for each other. At first they kept Friday nights to themselves. They got a sitter and went out for a simple dinner and sometimes a little dancing. Once a month or so they'd hook up with a larger crowd of friends, married and single, and stay out late — although almost never as late as they had routinely been out when they dated. Usually the sitter had to be home by midnight. So that was their curfew too. They joked about it. Being married, having children — and having a midnight curfew again. They laughed at the irony.

Besides, at least one of the kids was always up at daybreak anyway, and they realized that it's a lot easier to fix breakfast for a demanding toddler when you're doing it on a full night's sleep. Life was pretty good for Tom and Michelle. With their big family, sometimes money was a little tight. But neither of them had extravagant tastes. And Michelle seemed to have a gift for stretching a dollar in the grocery store and the clothing shops.

Lately they had started saving up to replace their car with a mini-van to better accommodate their family's size. When Tom's dad asked them what they planned to buy, Tom replied, "Depends on what I can get the best deal on." When Tom's mom asked about options they'd like on the van, Michelle chimed in. "Four tires and hold the rust," she said, like she was ordering at a fast food drive-in. Everyone got a good chuckle about that. Even if money didn't grow on the trees in their yard, they wouldn't have traded places with anyone.

But Tom noticed how the children were finding other things besides him with which to fill their lives. So although he could see that his family circumstances were very different from Derek's, he could point to a common thread and respond sympathetically. "The early years were great, Derek. It was such a kick to be the center of their lives," Tom replied. "But those days are gone, aren't they? And they're never coming back." He shook his head and looked off wistfully. "Is that what's bothering you, Derek?" he asked. "Is it that you're not the center of your kids' lives anymore?"

Derek looked up and chuckled, resigned to that fact that his children didn't always put him first like they had when they were younger. "Yeah, it bothers me sometimes. But that's not really what's bothering me now, Tom. It's more than that. A lot more. I just wish I could get a better handle on it."

"You're doing fine. Don't stop now," Tom offered. "We'll get to the bottom of it. Take your time."

Derek looked him in the eye. "Thanks," he said. His tone was serious and sincere. "I knew I could come to you. I know we haven't been the closest friends, but on the other side of the equation I've known you for a good, long time and I figured you've always been steady. So here I am," he said, letting a little smile come to his lips.

"You're kind to say that," Tom replied. "I appreciate it. I really do. But let's get back to why we're here. Tell me more about what's bugging you." Derek sighed and settled deeper in his chair. It looked as if he was finally ready to pour his heart out and take his chances that he could get some help, some focus. "Okay, pal. Let's talk about me. But it's going to take a little time. I've got a lot of ground to cover."

"I'm all ears," Tom said with a wry smile. That gave them both a good chuckle, because it was true. Among Tom's many endowments were a very substantial set of ears. He had been teased about them plenty in school. But eventually he got over it. In fact, he even seemed to grow into them a little over the years. As long as Michelle didn't seem to mind, and the kids all got Michelle's petite little ears, he could live with his generous endowment. The little joke put Derek even more at ease. He was ready to open up, and it was still early. No one else would be showing up at work for nearly an hour.

DEREK'S STORY

"I'm not a bad guy, I'm really not," Derek began. "Okay, at least I don't think I am. For the moment I'll leave that up to you. As a practical matter, I guess we leave that up to a lot of people. Everybody we meet makes up their own mind. But hey, I've always been good at getting people to like me, and people aren't stupid, so I figure I must be a pretty good guy. Are you with me so far?" he asked Tom.

"Sure am," Tom said, nodding. He wanted to reassure Derek, but he didn't want to take the wind out of his sails.

"Okay, I'm not a bad guy," Derek repeated, "but I'm not a real good one either. And worst of all, when I try being a really good guy for a very long time, I lose it. I just don't stick with it. Know what I mean?"

"I think so, but can you be more specific?" Tom asked, still smiling and leaning forward to assure Derek that he was interested in what Derek had to say.

"All right, let's start with Sally. You know Sally. Well, maybe you don't know her well. But you've talked to her at the company Christmas party and summer picnic. You know she's a looker too, don't you? Everybody knows that. Maybe she's not as incredible as she was when we met 15 years ago, but she still stops traffic." Tom decided it was best not to respond directly. "So what about you and Sally?" he asked, subtly trying to move the discussion back to them as a couple.

Derek was wise to the ploy. He smiled. "You agree, she's beautiful. But never mind about that for the moment. I confess that when I first saw her, it was all physical. Even after we dated for a while, probably even when I asked her to marry me. I was just stunned by her looks and that's about all I thought about. Looking back I'm sure it helped that she's a really sweet person. Otherwise, I'm sure something would have happened to take my focus off her beauty. But it didn't, and I'm sure that's to her credit. Anyway, I both liked her and I liked showing her off. And over the years I think I have really come to love her."

Derek stopped to let that sink in. It was clear he was looking for some response. "What makes you say that?" Tom asked, keeping the focus on what Derek had to say.

"Well, there are a lot of reasons really," Tom replied. "One is sort of superficial, but hear me out. When we dated and even after we were first married, it bothered me to see her when she wasn't at her best. You know, in the morning, or after a bad day with the kids, or when she was getting ready to go out and was messing with her hair and makeup. It was better for me just to not be around any of that. So when I got up I'd kiss the back of her shoulder and just get moving. And when I came home if she was a little disheveled, I just looked the other way and found something else to occupy me — the paper or something like that. And when we were going out, I'd always get ready early, before she started, so I wouldn't have to see any of the preparation.

"But now, Tom, it's like none of that bothers me. I like saying good morning to her and giving her a big kiss, even if her hair is all over the place and she doesn't have any lipstick on. And when I get back from a trip, I just love to hug her and kiss her. It doesn't matter what she looks like. Just last week, when I came home she was working in the flower garden. When she stood up her hair was a mess and there was dirt on her nose and chin. But I didn't care. You know what I did? I gave her a big hug and kiss without realizing that she was covered in wet potting soil. I hope the cleaners can salvage that suit. But at the time I didn't care. Still don't. I was just happy to be holding her. Do you think that's all superficial, or do you think that's a sign that I love her?"

Tom suddenly felt just a little playful. "I think it could it be both," he said. When Derek didn't laugh, Tom quickly added. "You know, it could be superficial but also an important sign that you really love her — and that your love for her is growing deeper. I mean, we're both normal, and it's normal for a man to notice and to like a pretty woman when we see one. But we also know that focusing only on beauty is superficial. And I think we also both know how dangerous that can be. Remember Todd and Janice?

Derek's eyes brightened. He was ready to take a quick break from his own concerns. "Todd and Janice! Man, I had forgotten them. But you're right. I mean, they were the best looking couple in the whole school. All the girls hated her, but they also talked about how incredibly awesome their kids would look if they ever got married."

"Yeah," Tom chimed in. And all the guys talked about how it would be such a shame if Todd fell down a manhole and disappeared and someone had to comfort Janice for her loss."

"You're right!" Derek added. "We all thought that was a match made in heaven. But how long did the marriage last? A year?"

"Not that long," Tom offered. "And if you're talking about a *happy* marriage, I'm not sure it lasted through the first night. I remember how they were arguing as they drove off on their honeymoon, and then they were back in a few days — not speaking to each other except, I'm told, to yell and scream. They never spent any time together after that and in less than a year, they were divorced."

"Whatever happened to them?" asked Derek.

"I'm not sure about Janice," Tom replied. "Todd ended up enlisting and making the military a career. I hear he's an officer serving in Europe, and that he has a wife and a couple of kids. I guess he's doing okay. Janice took off for New York to pursue a modeling career. I never heard a thing after that."

"Yeah, the girls never talked much about her, and they sure didn't want us guys talking about her either," Derek nodded. "So I never asked. But I always wondered. She must have changed her name when she went to New York."

"Why do you say that?" Tom asked.

"Oh, I tried to look her up the first couple of times I went there on business," Derek replied. "But I couldn't find her in the phone book and directory assistance had nothing." Suddenly he interrupted himself. "Look, nothing happened. I never saw her and there's no reason to think anything would have happened if I did. Just an old classmate."

"Right," said Tom."

"Okay, so I admit I was curious, I was attracted. But I can assure you, I was not looking for a permanent relationship. Behind her beauty was a very, very difficult person to be around. In fact, I told Todd that before they were married, and he brought it up once when we bumped into each other after they separated. But on those trips to New York, I asked myself: What can be the harm in a little dinner, maybe a drink or two?"

"You were still single, right?" Tom asked.

"Not exactly," Derek replied a little sheepishly. "This was a couple of years after Sally and I tied the knot. I don't know what I was thinking. Okay, I was thinking she was a real beauty and it might be fun to spend a little time with her in New York. Maybe she had changed. Maybe she was easier to get along with. I confess, the whole idea had some appeal. Look, I said I was a pretty good guy, not a saint. Maybe that wasn't my best idea, but you know, I've never really cheated on Sally — not even once in our entire marriage."

"A lot of men can't say that," Tom offered, trying to get the discussion back on a more positive track.

"Well, I can," Derek said. "But I also have to admit it's been close a couple of times. Usually I use pretty good judgment. But there have been a couple of times that scared even me. Most of them were pretty early in our marriage when I guess I was still getting used to the idea of having an exclusive relationship with one person. But you know, from time to time I still get a little frisky. The difference is that now I don't go looking for the opportunity. I don't want to be attracted to other women. So when it happens — and I admit it happened just last week — it bothered me. I thought about it a lot, and I decided that I'm at a point in my life where I'd like to be better than that.

"You know," Derek continued, "I've never liked being average. In fact, I don't think I ever have been average —

unless you count my grades in college, when I was busy trying not to be average in other areas, if you get my drift. Anyway, I thought about it after not pursuing that beautiful woman last week and I decided that I'd like to be a better husband and father than the run of the mill pond scum that's so common out there. Believe me, I don't want to end up like Gene in marketing. I hear he lost everything — wife, kids, house — over one little fling."

"That's right, he did," said Tom. "I don't like to tell tales out of school, but he has made no secret of it. In fact, he's become quite an apostle for fidelity. He tells everyone he can. He even has a little ditty that he shares with whomever will listen. *'Do as I say, not as I do — to keep the family, the house and your Beemer too.'* It's killing him, but I think he figures he got what he deserved. And I guess it's to his credit that he wants things to turn out better for his friends," Tom offered.

"Yeah, I heard him go on about it at lunch the other day," Derek said. "In a way, I guess that's part of what prompted me to come up and see you. Gene made me see that occasionally I've been playing with fire, and though I haven't been burned, it could happen if I don't shape up. Like I said, I'm not a bad guy. But I have lived near the edge, and after listening to Gene that scares me. I'm worried about something else too. I'm concerned that my home life may come apart — really just fizzle away — even if I am a good boy on the road. We need a good dose of something, maybe love, maybe just friendship or even a little consideration would help. And I know I should be leading the way. So I know I ought to change somehow. But I guess I don't know what to change or how to change. And truth be told, I guess

I'd like a better reason to change than fear. I'd like something positive to point to. As a salesman, I've always responded to goals. So I guess I'd like a goal to motivate me to change so I'm not at risk."

"What about Sally, her happiness and your marriage? Aren't those worthy goals for you?" Tom asked.

"Sure, they're worthy. And I cherish them. It's the same with the kids. And with the house and the Beemer and all the other toys I've accumulated over the years too. I hate to admit it, but I like having it all. Tom, you've got to believe me, Sally and the kids mean *a lot more* to me than the house and car. But I confess, it all matters to me. That said, I have to admit that the thought of just hanging on to what I have just doesn't seem to work as an effective goal for me. I'm ashamed to admit it, but what motivates me is *more* — always more."

The room was quiet. Tom wanted to fill the space, to encourage Derek to go on, but he had to stop and think for a minute. "What about the idea of making yourself a better person, the kind of person your wife and kids could really look up to, that they could really count on, no matter what the circumstances? How would you like to go to sleep every night, no matter whether you were at home or on the road, knowing that you had provided for them by giving them a person like that to look after them — and that person would be *you?* Would that motivate you to change?"

Derek looked past Tom, out the window and across the skyline. He was quiet for what seemed like a long time. Then he spoke, almost in a whisper. "It could, Tom. I think it could. Yes, I'm pretty sure. But I don't know where to begin.

Life doesn't come with many guarantees. That would be a pretty substantial one."

"Yes, it would, Derek," Tom replied. "But maybe we're on to something. What else is bothering you?"

"Well, that's a big part of it — what we've been talking about," Derek replied, speaking more quickly and earnestly. "It's hard to put into words but, well, as I said before, I think I'm a pretty good guy. But I would like to be a better guy. More stable. More anchored. More dependable. More reliable. I'd like to be able to trust myself more. I'd like to know, no matter what the circumstances, that I really will do the right thing rather than the easy thing or the fun thing or the lazy thing.

"I mean, I'm a pretty good father. But you know what? The kids are drifting away from me — and not just because they are growing up and developing normally. I know that their worlds are quickly becoming a lot bigger than just mom and dad. And if that were all there is to it, I would still be a little disappointed. But I wouldn't feel like I do now. I'm sure that part of the reason that the kids are drifting away from me is that I don't spend enough time with them. Of course, you know that I travel. And when I get home, I'm tired and I want to relax. So for a long time I've been able to blame my job. But lately I know better.

"I know part of it is that when I am home, I'm busy with other things — the paper, magazines, sports on TV, making plans and doing things with my own friends. I say that I'm tired when I get home from a trip. But I always find time to go hunting and fishing with my buddies. I just can't seem to find the time to take my own kids fishing. That's starting to bother me. I'm disappointed in myself. About six months ago I set a goal to spend at least one full day every other weekend doing something with Sally and the kids — or just with the kids if what Sally needed most was a break from them."

"How'd you do with that," Tom asked, interested in Derek's answer as much for his own sake as for Derek's.

"I did great!" Derek replied. "Sally was all excited about my goal, and the very next weekend we arranged to spend the day at the zoo. It's about an hour and a half's drive from home, so we packed a big picnic lunch and decided to make a full day of it. You know, we got that picnic basket for our wedding. I don't know how many years it had been since we had it out. I had nearly forgotten about the thing. But it was perfect for our trip to the zoo, and we had a ball.

"I had no idea the kids knew so much. Our oldest went on and on about the life cycle of polar bears. She knew way more than I ever imagined anyone could know. And our little guy — I was amazed that he knew the name of practically every animal. The only one that really stumped him was the zebra. He asked me, 'Daddy, is that horse in jail?' As first I didn't get it, but Sally said they had seen a comedy on TV where these prisoners had on striped uniforms. It cracked me up. And you should hear him say 'hippopotamus.' It's not perfect, but it is priceless.

"Tom, I can't remember when I was as happy as I was that day. And Sally looked at me the whole time the way she did when we were dating. I felt like royalty. Like a king. And the kids had just as much fun. After the zoo we stopped for pizza and the kids convinced me to take everyone to a movie. I asked them, 'Haven't you had enough?' And you know what they said? The oldest chanted, almost shouting,

'No, no, no, we want a show.' Then they all started to repeat the chant. Even Sally. Everybody in the place started to look over at us, and I thought the owner was going to throw us out. I was just about to furrow my brow, like I do so often, and tell them firmly to knock it off when I got an epiphany."

"What was that?" Tom asked.

"I told them 'yes, let's do it.' They all cheered for a few seconds, until I told them they had to pick a movie. That's when they got serious and everyone quieted down. I got them a paper, we found a good Disney feature we all agreed would be fine, and some of us even stayed awake until it was over."

Tom couldn't resist. "And you, Derek, did you stay awake until the end?"

"Almost," said Derek, laughing. "But, of course, the kids teased me about that all the way home. 'Daddy's up past his bedtime,' they taunted, and that gave us some more good laughs. Honestly, it was the best day I can remember in a long, long time — maybe back to when I first started dating Sally and we were so young and carefree. Anyway, it was great. It started out great."

"And after that?" Tom asked.

"Hmm," Derek replied. "Let's see. Since my goal was to have a day's outing every two weekends and we had achieved it right away, we really had three weekends to schedule our next family day.

"Where did you go the next time?" Tom asked.

"There hasn't been a next time," Derek replied, letting his head tilt downward. "Let's see. We purposely took the next weekend off. Then the following weekend there was the big football game at our alma mater downstate, so I went with some friends and we stayed down overnight. But I didn't worry. We still had one more weekend to meet my goal and stay on track. Only we planned to go to the amusement park the next weekend and it rained both days."

"What did you do then?" Tom asked.

"On the first day of the weekend I urged patience and promised better things the next day. When it was still raining the second day, I rented some videos and Sally popped some popcorn and we tried to make the day special. But then I got a call from my brother, and that took a while, and Sally had to do some shopping for the kids for school, and next thing we knew, we were yelling for the kids to finish their homework and go to bed. I felt terrible, but I promised the kids we would catch up with three things over the next four weeks."

"But that didn't work out?" Tom asked, sure of the answer but interested in giving Derek a chance to share the details.

"The first weekend some buddies had planned a fishing trip, and I didn't panic because I knew we could get in all I had promised over the next three weekends. But I forgot that I had promised my dad I would go over to his place and paint his garage, which took both days of the next weekend. The next weekend I wasn't slated to get home from a business trip until mid-day Saturday, but I still had Sunday — until our oldest child's team qualified for a tournament out of town. I thought we could turn that into a family day, but her team kept winning and they played three games that day, so we just sat in the stands and cheered her on. She was thrilled, but the other kids felt betrayed.

"The next weekend was Sally's sister's birthday, and we always drive over there for that. It's a five-hour trip, so we spent that weekend in the car and socializing with Sally's family, which meant we really didn't have any time to do something special with the kids. As the next weekend approached, I tried to get the kids up for something but they weren't interested. The oldest said, 'Forget it, Dad. We don't want to get excited planning anything. Something will just come up and we'll be more disappointed than if we just don't think about it.' I was hurt, even a little angry. But the kids were right. I don't even remember what went wrong now, but we never did get around to doing anything, and I've been afraid to even bring up the idea since then."

"So you're pretty disappointed in yourself?" Tom asked.

"Yeah, and I'm not the only one," Derek replied. "I find myself thinking that maybe it would have been better if I hadn't even suggested the idea in the first place. I mean, that first day was great beyond words. But now I wonder if it was even worth the long-range fallout. So yeah, we're all disappointed in dear old dad. And you know what else? I really feel stupid. If I hadn't suggested it in the first place, it wouldn't be a problem now. And if I hadn't made some dumb and lazy decisions after that, it wouldn't be a problem either. I could blame work — I did that one weekend when I was late getting back into town. But that just made me feel more stupid. I mean, how can I blame one late plane for four weekends of fumbled goals? I wish I could. But it's my fault pure and simple. I don't like acknowledging that, but what choice do I have? Besides, it's not news to anyone else in my family."

"So, you're disappointed in yourself as a husband and a father?" Tom asked, figuring it was time to try to recap what Derek had been sharing with him. "You're not a bad guy, as you say, but you could be a lot better. You *want* to be a lot better. You have even *tried* to be a lot better. In fact, occasionally you have *succeeded,* and when that happened, you enjoyed it and felt good about yourself. And can I assume that you quit trying to locate Janice?"

"You assume right — about Janice and about everything else," Derek replied. "I'm not a bad father or a bad husband. But I'm not a super star either. And you know what, Tom? Frankly, I don't want this to sound too egotistical, but I have been pretty darn good — near the top of the heap — with everything else in life. I think it's fair to say I'm what they call a 'high achiever.' So frankly, I'm having trouble with myself not being one in my roles as husband and father right now. My fumbling the ball as a father amounted to fumbling the ball as a husband too, because Sally got almost all of the fallout from the kids' disappointment. She didn't say it exactly, but I'm pretty sure that's mostly what they've all talked about when I've been on the road."

"So you're feeling pretty low right now — is that right?" Tom asked.

"Yeah, I feel low," Derek replied. "And I'm confused too. How come I'm such a high achiever in so many areas and then, when it comes to my wife and kids, I'm such a loser? And why, when I try to improve things, can't I stick to my goals and get it done like I do in other areas of life?"

Tom thought it was time to answer Derek's questions with a question of his own. "Derek, those are some big questions you've put on the table. But before we try to answer them, can I slip in a couple too?" he asked.

"Go for it," Derek replied.

"Derek, do you believe in God?" Tom asked.

Derek let out a nervous little chuckle and the question caused his brow to furrow, like he was confused by Tom's tack. "Yeah, sure. Doesn't everybody?" he replied. He was obviously uneasy with the direction in which the discussion was going.

Tom decided to take a little edge off his line of inquiry. "I think you're right," he declared with a big smile. "Most everybody in this country does believe in God. I think the figure is about 95 percent."

"Just like you accountant guys to quantify everything," Derek teased.

His smile told Tom it was okay to proceed to the next question. "Yeah, once an accountant always an accountant," Tom agreed, eager to keep the mood light as he asked his next question. "So you believe in God. Do you belong to a church and attend regularly?"

Derek squirmed in his chair, obviously uneasy with the question. "No, we don't belong or go to church," he said, carefully choosing the plural *we* to take any onus off himself personally. "But who does anymore? Our parents are pretty active in churches, but Sally and I were just never into that very much. And what does that have to do with anything we've been talking about?" There was an edge to his obviously rhetorical question.

Tom smiled and leaned forward, anxious to keep the tone of the conversation open and not defensive. "You're right again, Tom. A lot of people don't go to church these days. If you'll forgive the accountant in me, I'll concede that the number of people who don't attend regularly exceeds the number who do. More than half belong to a church, but less than half are in church on any given Sunday."

Derek was still a little uneasy, and ready to move the conversation to another topic. "Thanks for the update, Tom," he said with a grin. "But I don't see where any of this talk about God and church is taking us anywhere. Can we get back to the issue we were talking about a few minutes ago?"

"The issue of *you?*" Tom asked, careful to smile and arch his eyebrows so as not to let his words sound too harsh.

"Yeah, if you want to put it that way — the issue of me," Derek agreed. "So can we get back to that? We don't have much more time," he said, glancing at his watch.

"Fair enough, Derek," Tom replied. "You came to me as an old friend, hoping that I would hear you out and help you with some personal issues. I'm honored that you would do that, and I really hope I can be of some help. The only point I'm making at the moment is that eventually — and you know this — you've got to help yourself. So the best way I can help you is to help bring you to the point where you can be of more help to yourself."

"You're right about that," Derek said. "I do have to help myself. And that's the kind of help I came here to get, I guess. So why, all of a sudden, all this talk about God and church? Do you really think those things can make any difference with the things we've been talking about in my life?"

Derek was more relaxed again, and that restored the mood of two old friends just talking — even if the term *old friends* was stretching the truth just a bit. Tom saw that

Derek's question was giving him an opportunity, and he took it. "Derek, I'm convinced that God and church can make a difference with issues like the ones you've been sharing with me today. In fact, I think they can make a *huge* difference. I'm basing my conviction on personal experience and the experiences of many people I know. However, what's important at the end of the day is not what I think, but what *you* think."

"Thanks for saying that," Derek interrupted, a big smile on his face. "I was afraid I was going to get one of those born again lectures like the ones I hear parts of when I'm surfing the cable channels. Frankly, they don't do anything for me."

"I didn't think they would," Tom smiled back at Derek. "Frankly, I keep surfing too until I find a sports channel or a cop show. But if you respect my judgment — and I think that's what you were saying when you came up here today — I hope you will let me try to help you answer your own questions by tossing out a couple of questions about faith and church. That's all I'm asking. Is that reasonable?" He leaned forward and let a large smile cross his face.

"Okay, it's reasonable," Derek replied. "I trust that you're not going to preach to me or try to convert me or save me or whatever it is that you churchgoers do. So where do we start?" Derek asked. "Just don't ask me to go to church with you this Sunday. I've got a big golf date set up. And even if I didn't, I could arrange one pretty quick if my only option was to spend the morning in church. No church, okay?"

"I won't ask you to do *anything* associated with church," Tom replied. "All I want you to do is to meet some people right here in the building and share your skepticism with them. If, when you're done, nobody has been any help, we'll work out a different plan to try to get and keep you on track with your spouse and children. Is that fair?"

"Yeah, it's fair. But why don't we just get busy with the different plan now and forget the other stuff?" Derek wondered out loud.

"Good question," Tom replied. "But I have a good answer. You said your problem wasn't knowing what to do. You know what to do. And you had a plan. But you didn't stick with it. And you told me that was pretty much the pattern. With work issues, you make a plan, you set goals, you reach or exceed those goals, you get the gold. Then you make more and bigger plans with higher and higher goals, always pushing up the bar in the company's sales force, always setting the standard.

"But at home, with your wife and kids, it's different. You make a plan but you don't reach your goals. All I want you to do is to ask some people around here how they do better in their personal lives, especially on the home front. After you've heard them out, you decide if there's anything there to help you achieve your goals off the job. You're a smart guy. I think you can get a lot out of what these folks have to say. But it's up to you."

"All right, let's try it your way for a while," Derek said. "When do we begin?"

Derek's can-do attitude was never far from the surface, even when things seemed to be going badly. Tom liked that quality in Derek — in fact, he wished he had more of it himself. He was counting on Derek's energy and drive to get him through the series of encounters he was preparing to arrange for Derek.

"Why don't you see Jerry in marketing first? I know he's in the building all week. Why don't I call him and ask him to contact you to find a good time to get together?"

"You're not going to tell him about my problems, are you?" Derek asked in earnest. Suddenly he was very nervous about the whole idea.

"No," Tom replied. "All I'm going to tell him is that you and I were talking about God and church, faith and religion, and you asked me how they could be any good to anyone. I'll tell him you're a skeptic — a great and warm and friendly skeptic — who has agreed to discuss his skepticism. How's that?"

"That's fine," said Derek, still obviously a little wary. "I'll wait for him to call. But you're not off the hook yet, old pal," he added as he stood to leave.

"Good!" Tom said enthusiastically. "Because I don't want to be off the hook. Talk with Jerry and get back to me. I really do want to help."

"Thanks," Derek said softly. "I believe you do. It wasn't easy coming here, so thanks for making me feel welcome."

"No problem," Tom said, reaching out his hand. "Get back to me as soon as you've seen Jerry. I'll be waiting for you." Derek shook his hand, winked and headed out the door. "Thanks again, pal. I knew I could count on you," he said as he stepped into the hallway and headed for the elevator. When the elevators doors opened, there was a big rush of people getting off. Derek disappeared into the herd and the elevator door closed. Tom picked up the phone to call Jerry and ask him to meet with Derek.

JERRY'S STORY

Within 10 minutes of getting back to his desk, Derek got an e-mail message from Jerry saying they could meet anytime in the next two days. Derek replied that he'd like to get together about 3 p.m. that same day, and Jerry's almost immediate response was, "I'm looking forward to making your acquaintance."

A few minutes before 3 p.m. Derek got off the elevator at the third floor, turned right and headed down the hallway toward marketing. At the reception desk a young woman greeted him with a big smile. Since he was wearing his company badge, she could see his name and knew exactly what to do. "Good afternoon. Are you the Derek that Jerry's expecting?"

"Yes I am," Derek responded with a big smile of his own. Ordinarily he would have flirted with her. Nothing much ever came of his flirtations, but as he liked to say to his buddies, "You never know." Still, under the circumstances, flirting struck him as inappropriate. "Second door on the left," the receptionist said, pointing and still smiling. Derek nodded and quickly moved down the hall to Jerry's office. At the doorway, Jerry noticed him and said, "Derek, come in." He stood up, stepped around his desk, extended his hand and said, "I'm glad you could see me so quickly."

"That was going to be my line," Derek said as he shook Jerry's hand. His dad had taught him the importance of a good, firm handshake in leaving a strong impression on everyone he met. It seemed to serve him well.

"Sit down," Jerry said as he motioned to one of two comfortable chairs in the corner. "Can I get you anything?" When Derek shook his head no, Jerry sat down in the other comfortable chair and asked, "So what can I do for you?"

Derek was not at ease. But he had made enough cold calls in his life to quickly take control with a question of his own. "What did Tom tell you?" he asked.

"Tom said you had been in to see him and the conversation had turned to issues of religious belief and practice. At some point he thought my story might be helpful to you, and he asked if I would set up an appointment to discuss my journey with you," Jerry replied in a friendly tone.

"Your journey? I'm not sure I understand that," said Derek, still not sure if he was going to be comfortable with this process. In all his life, he had never sat and talked with another man about God or faith or church or anything related to any of those matters.

Jerry replied, "Sorry, Derek, I'm getting ahead of myself. Sometimes I do that. Being in marketing, I should know better. But sometimes I forget it. My reference to 'journey' reveals my fundamental belief that life here on earth is a faith journey — some would say a 'pilgrimage.' It's the same thing. I believe that my largest purpose is to serve God, and the way I do that is to grow as a disciple of Christ. So life for me is a journey that permits me to get closer to God every day."

"Heavy stuff," said Derek, not sure exactly what to say.

"Don't let me put you off, Derek," Jerry responded with a smile. "My experience of myself is that I'm a sinner. My journey involves a lot of stumbles and not a few falls. I drift. I stray. It's a struggle. But I'm trying. You might call me a *Christian under construction.*"

"Interesting phrase," said Derek, repeating it. *"A Christian under construction.* When I think back to my days as a kid in Sunday school, I guess I was that too. But I just figured there came a point when the process stopped. You know, some people turn out to be finished products. Then they do their thing on Sunday mornings in church while the rest of us do our thing at the *Church of the Inner Spring* or the *Church with 19 Holes.*"

Jerry chuckled. *"The Church of the Inner Spring* and the *Church with 19 Holes.* I hadn't heard those terms before. But you know, I've been a faithful member of both of those congregations in my time. Especially the first. Looking back, I'd have to say that I've spent more Sunday mornings in bed than in church. But those days are behind me now, and I feel blessed."

Derek cut in. "Yeah, Tom says you go to church regularly and also are part of some Bible study and prayer group here in the building. I have to confess, I just don't get it. But hey, I'm asking. How did you get from the *Church of the Inner Spring* to where you are today?"

Jerry smiled and leaned toward Derek. "I'm glad you're asking. I'm always happy to share my story. It's really pretty simple. Let me put this in sales terms for a minute if I can. Like you, I grew up with Sunday school and church services, so I was exposed to all the *features* of my Christian faith tradition. But I have to tell you, as far back as I can remember I didn't see any *benefits.* So as soon as I got out of the house and headed to college, I said goodbye to church and hello to those inner springs. It was that way for years. And I have to admit, I was pretty content.

"I got married," Jerry continued. "Sandy was a sweet girl. She really swept me off my feet. She was a regular churchgoer, but she didn't prod me to go — at least not after the wedding ceremony. That was a big church affair. It was probably the only big, lavish event that ever mattered to her. After that she went to church regularly and I stayed home. She would ask me to go from time to time, always very sweetly. But I'd tell her I had a date: Me, the Sunday paper, and a hot cup of coffee. Then the kids came along and I marketed myself as a convenient babysitter. I looked at the time she was in church as good time for me to spend alone with the kids. And I think she appreciated a little time alone without the kids hanging on her — although being a good mother was so important to her that I don't think she'd ever admit that."

Derek was unsure why Jerry spoke of Sandy in the past tense. Surely, Jerry had great love and affection for his wife, and the couple couldn't be more than 50 years old. He almost asked about it, but then decided to ask a more general question. "So for a while she went to church and you stayed home with the kids, building up your brownie points as a father and husband?"

"I did while the kids were small," he replied. "Then gradually, as each approached school age, Sandy started taking them to church and Sunday school. Sometimes, as a necessity, I got involved as a chauffeur or I showed up with the family for big occasions. And we all went to church together on Christmas and Easter. But gradually the kids all ended up in church with her and I was alone again. That's when I started to attend the *Church with 19 Holes,* as you call it. Sandy was good with that too. I mean, she would ask me from time to time if I wanted to go with her and the kids, but she never pushed it."

"But that's not the end of the story, obviously, or we wouldn't be having this conversation," Derek chimed in, anxious to show that he was a pretty savvy guy.

"No, that's not the end of the story. In fact, the story doesn't have any end — at least not yet," Jerry teased. "But it does have a few turns before it gets to today, and when we get to today I'll stop." Both men chuckled as Jerry continued. "We had a good life, Derek. We really did. Sandy was always a sweetheart — and a friend too. And our children — we had three — are the loves of my life. They're grown now. The last one graduates from college next spring, and I'm sure she'll do fine. Wants to be a teacher.

"But I digress. We had a good life. I spent Sunday mornings on the golf course or with my paper and coffee. Sandy and the kids were good with that. Although as my son got older, it became a bigger chore for Sandy to get him up and dressed and off to church. He said he hated it. That it was boring. I tried to stay out of it because I knew how important it was to Sandy. But I also knew how the kid felt — just like me. So sometimes on Saturday night I'd ask about taking him with me to the golf course, and sometimes she agreed."

"So you were still a good dad, and a good husband for respecting Sandy's wishes," Derek offered.

"Yeah, I guess at one level I was a good father and husband — although looking back now I wish I had done some things differently. I won't bore you with the details. We were going along fine like I've described until Sandy got the diagnosis of breast cancer. That was a pretty big shock for all of us." Jerry's eyes got misty. He stopped talking for just a moment and looked down. He continued to look down as he started to speak again. "Sorry. It's still a little difficult to talk about," he said.

"We could pick this up at another time," Derek offered. "No, that's okay," Jerry replied. "I want to share my story. In fact, it helps. So you're doing me the favor today, Derek. Just bear with me a second."

In a moment Jerry looked up and continued. "Sandy's diagnosis of breast cancer just destroyed me. I didn't know where to turn. I didn't want to be an added burden on her, but I confess, I was so torn up I wasn't much good supporting her. So when we needed communication the most, it pretty much broke down. For the first few days, I was pretty tender, all tears and sobs. She was my *life,* my reason for *living.* How could this be happening to *me?* Then the anger took over. I was angry at the cancer. I was angry at Sandy for having cancer. I was angry with our children for the way they handled it. Things got hopeless for me pretty quickly. I really hit the skids. I wanted to be more supportive but I wanted relief too. I spent more time at what you call the 19th hole, even when I didn't golf. I let myself get busier at work. I stayed late. I took a couple of trips that weren't absolutely necessary. I tried to look busy, but I pretty much fell apart and wallowed in self-pity," Jerry said, a look of beaten resignation on his face.

"I'll bet Sandy was a mess too," Derek offered.

"No, that's the strange part, Derek. She was a rock through the whole ordeal. She was so steady and stable and hopeful through all the treatments. When she lost her hair, she joked about it. Remember that chrome-domed actor Yul Brynner? Maybe that's before your time. He starred in *The King and I,* a Broadway musical by Rogers and Hammerstein adapted from Margaret Landon's novel, *Anna and the King of Siam.* Later Brynner starred in a movie version with Deborah Kerr and his role became a classic. So Sandy would ask if America was ready for her remake, *The Queen and I.* And she joked that she was going to enter the WNBA draft as Michelle Jordan. Sometimes the whole thing could be just too bittersweet and we'd ask her to stop. But she was a trouper to the end."

"The end?" asked Derek, almost inadvertently. As soon as he said it, he wished he had kept his big mouth shut.

"Yes, Sandy died three years ago. I won't kid you. It's been a struggle. In fact, I don't know how I would have gotten through it without my faith."

"Your faith?" Derek blurted, again wishing he'd just kept quiet.

But Jerry produced a big, broad smile and nodded his head several times. "Yes, my faith," he said. "I think of it now as Sandy's legacy to me, and so I appreciate it all the more. It's what's saved me, Derek, here and now. I can't explain it any other way." But the baffled look on Derek's face said Jerry had to fill in a lot more details, and pretty quickly.

"As I was saying," Jerry quickly continued, "I fell apart while Sandy stayed on course — even though it was *her* problem. Anyway, my guilt piled up and up as she just kept on course. Oh, once in a while she would break down a bit. But always, it was out of this sense that she didn't want to abandon the kids. That bothered her more than anything. And she wanted to be assured that I could handle things if she was gone — which, of course, for a while I gave absolutely no indication I was capable of doing. But as the days went by and I sunk lower and lower and our relationship deteriorated, she reached out more and more to me, trying to support me. Finally I just couldn't take it anymore. I guess you could say I blew up and broke down all at the same time. The kids were all staying with friends that night, so we had the run of the house, and we used it.

"I won't go into all the details," Jerry continued, "but we got a lot out on the table that night. Near the end she said she learned that I wasn't quite full of despair as she had feared, and that gave her hope. She said it was an answer to her prayers. And I learned that she wasn't quite the Rock of Gibraltar I had been seeing. I learned that she was going through everything I was going through — and some of it more intensely than I was, no doubt because *she* had the illness and was looking at her own death. But the difference between us was that she wasn't going through it alone."

Derek was intrigued. "What do you mean, she wasn't going through it alone. With whom was she going through it?"

"With God, Derek. With Jesus Christ. She was walking *with* the Lord, Derek, while I was torn between doubting there was a God and wanting to punch him in the mouth. Here I was, a bystander, cursing God, saying things like, 'If you exist, how can you be doing this? How can you let it happen? If you can prevent this and don't, I want nothing to do with you.' But there was Sandy, the victim, going on about how she's so grateful to be walking with the Lord, and how she really has a sense that he is holding her hand! Derek, I was just amazed. Baffled, really."

Derek cut in. "Thanks for saying that — baffled. I guess I am too. How could she feel closer to God if God was letting her suffer so much? I just don't get it."

"I didn't get it either, Derek. And let me add, it took a long, long time before I started to get it — even a little bit. But I'm an empiricist, and there was something I couldn't deny. She had it together and I didn't. And the difference was her faith. So I had to deal with that."

"Now I'm intrigued again," Derek said. "How did you, as you say, *deal with it?*"

"I'm not sure, exactly. What I know was that it was a process, not an instant conviction. I started with what was there. I told Sandy, 'I don't get it, honey. I just don't get it. I'm mad at God — hell, I'm mad at Creator and creation alike — and you're grateful to him. What's that all about? Where is it coming from?"

"What did she tell you?" Derek said with more than a little eagerness.

"Not much," Jerry replied with a smile. "What she said was that she understood that I didn't understand and that was okay. She said it was normal. But then she offered me an invitation. She asked me if I wanted to try to understand. What could I say? I was desperate. And I loved her. So I said 'yes' not really knowing exactly what I was agreeing to. I made a joke. "It won't hurt, will it?" I teased. "Not if you don't resist me," she joked right back as she took me in her arms."

Jerry's eyes focused beyond the room and his lips closed into a soft smile. Then he was back in the moment. "It was a good night, Derek, a really good night. We covered a lot of ground and ended up a lot closer than we had ever been before. Looking back, I have to say that things have never been quite the same since that night — and I mean that in a good sense, although certainly a lot of terrible things have happened. But after that, no matter what happened, I felt they happened to us together. Even her parting. I know we each go on alone in one sense. The feeling of loss was awful, for me and for the kids — and I had to be there for them as much as I could through that awful time. But it was not all bad. Most important, since that night I have never felt alone either. I still have this sense that she is here with me. Sometimes that hurts more than it heals, but overall it's a very comforting feeling. And through it all, right through today, I feel God's presence in my life. I am not alone, and I haven't been since that night."

Jerry took a deep breath and looked Derek in the eye. "I said the story doesn't have an end yet, but I'd stop when I got to today. I guess I'm there."

Derek chuckled nervously. He wasn't quite sure where to take the conversation, but he wasn't ready for it to end. "Listen," he said, "every good speaker takes questions at the end, and you're a good speaker, so you owe me, okay?

Besides, you still haven't answered the question I asked before."

"Oops, sorry, Derek. I got so caught up in my story I forgot what your question was. Will you give it to me again?" Derek was happy to oblige. "I asked, 'How could she feel closer to God if God was letting her suffer so much?' I said I didn't get it and I'm afraid I still don't."

"I'm sorry, Derek, I didn't mean to blow off that question. It's a good one and it deserves an answer. But recall that I said I'm just a *Christian under construction,* and I have to admit that this construction project is in the very early stages. I know faith was Sandy's source of strength, and I know once I accepted that and agreed to join her on her faith journey — go to church, go to a Bible study class once a week, pray with her every night and morning — I just know that somehow my life started to come together for me, just as Sandy's always stayed together for her.

"There's one other thing I should mention too," Jerry continued, "and that's the support of her faith community. People from her church were there for us every step of the way. The whole ordeal brought our own families closer together. But they could only do so much. Fortunately, members of her church were always there for us. They brought food to the house night after night. When I had to be out of town or couldn't miss an important meeting, members took Sandy to her treatments. One woman came over and fixed her nails. And you know what mattered most, Derek? They were always available to pray with us. At first that made me feel uncomfortable. But as I noticed what it did for Sandy — how it brought her so much peace — I felt more comfortable. Near the end, I was happy to join them.

And now that Sandy's gone, her faith community — *our* faith community — is a real anchor for me.

"I won't deny I had my period of darkness, a time where my sorrow was so deep that I tried to turn away from everything, to reject it, and crawl into a little hole of self-pity. I was there, or heading there. But a few members of our congregation handled that period beautifully. They were so understanding and so gentle. They brought me back from that brink of hopelessness and despair. I admit, I still catch myself going there. But when I do, I know I don't have to pull back with just my own strength. It's hard to put into words, but I just have this sense that they're there for me — and they always are.

"My story wouldn't be complete if I didn't note how Sandy's faith community really made a difference in our lives. I watched how Sandy's faith and her faith community really made a difference in her life. Gradually, those two things made a difference in my life. You know, Derek, in the last few months that she lived, I got to plumb the depths of Sandy's faith, and what I found was a deep well of life-giving nourishment. Again, it's hard to explain. But it was there. And it got her through this — it got both of us through it."

Jerry paused for a moment and then continued. "I'm sorry I don't have a handle on many of the *whys* yet. I just know the *whats* — what I saw in Sandy, what I've felt in my own life. I don't want to get maudlin, but there is one more thing I want to share with you. Sandy's last words were, 'Give it your best, Bubba. I love you and I'll see you soon enough.' That's what she told me every morning when I went out the door to work. And that's what she said at the end. Why? Because it wasn't the end for her. For her death was just one more step in a continuing process called life — and it's not over yet. As I said, I don't know the *whys,* but I know what I saw and what I feel to this day."

Jerry ended his little monologue by raising his hands, palms out, in the gesture of resignation. But the smile and the warmth in his eyes indicated he didn't feel helpless. Clearly he was at peace with where his faith journey had taken him. Derek was moved to speak. "That's quite a story, Jerry. I really appreciate your sharing it with me. But if you don't mind one more question, where do you think it will all go for you from here?"

Jerry was ready for the question. "I don't know that either, except to say I'm convinced that it is going some place. Life does have a point. Every life has a purpose. I'm not sure what mine is — except to try with all my might to be a good father and a faithful steward of all that God has given me. You know, there was a time when Sandy was sick and I was in such pain that I wondered if life might have been better if I had never met her at all. I struggled with that for quite a while. Know what I think now? I'm grateful for every moment God gave me with Sandy, and I'm grateful we still have each other, even though I miss her beyond what words can say. And I don't have words to express how grateful I am for the children God gave us. Sometimes I even catch myself being grateful for my job here, although you know there's been very little to celebrate in my department for a long, long time."

"Grateful for your job here?" Derek parroted Jerry, glad to have something light with which to close the conversation. "That's something! Hey, thanks again. Just one more thing. Where do I go to get my *whys* answered?"

"I'm not sure," Jerry replied. "But stay with it. Which reminds me, Tom told me to ask you to stop by and see him again after you were done with me. You know those accounting guys. They never leave the building."

"Yeah, they're like the carpet, I think. And just as exciting," Derek joked. "I've got a call to make this afternoon, so I might not get back to him today. But if you see him before I do, tell him he's on my short list. And thanks again. I have to confess, you've left me with a lot of questions. But I'm hopeful I'll get them answered," Derek said.

"Good," Jerry replied with a big smile. "And when you do, I hope you'll stop around and share your answers with me. As you can tell, I'm still a little short on answers myself."

A PRECIOUS GIFT

Back in his office, Derek's call went well and was over more quickly than he had anticipated. He decided to give Tom a quick try and picked up the phone. "Tom, here," came the response after just one ring. "What can I do for you?"

"It's Derek. I'm calling to thank you for setting up the meeting today with Jerry, and to ask if you have a few minutes before you leave the building today," Derek said.

"Sure, you know us accountants. I'll be around 'til five, regular as the clocks," Tom joked. "And I don't have any meetings today, so stop in any time."

"I'll see you about 4:30," said Derek, hanging up.

Derek was eager to see Tom, so he arrived a few minutes early. The receptionist recognized him and waved him toward Tom's office. "Hope I'm not too early and interrupting anything," he said as he stepped into Tom's office."

Tom looked up from his work and smiled. "Interrupting? No problem. This work will still be here when we're done — in fact, I think it will still be here when we're *gone,"* he said waving his hand to the pile of spreadsheets that covered his desk. "Thanks for coming by. I really need a break."

Derek liked to tease accountants, but he admired their attention to detail. That wasn't his strength. He called himself "a big picture guy" and he took pride in his ability to read a client, discern his needs and close the sale. But there were times when he had to admit a little more attention to detail would have come in handy — and maybe brought him a larger commission. So even though he didn't like anyone in accounting to question his expense reports, he did appreciate the fact that Tom and his colleagues did good work and seemed to keep the company on track in bad times as well as good. "It's dirty work but somebody has to do it," Derek said with more than his usual sincerity.

Tom chuckled and motioned Derek to take a seat. "I'm glad to hear your meeting with Jerry went well," he said. "And apparently, we didn't scare you off because here you are, eager to keep going. What else can I do for you?"

"Well, eager is too strong a word," said Derek. "But I am intrigued. Jerry has a powerful story to tell. It's so sad. And yet, it's not only sad. There's also a tale of redemption there, so to speak. But most of all, I have to confess that I'm impressed with how he has held up through it all. I don't know how I could deal with something like that. Maybe I haven't been the perfect husband, but the loss of Sally would be devastating. I can't imagine myself getting through it, and I hope I never have to. But that's not what I called you to discuss."

Tom had no trouble leaving talk of widowhood behind. He too marveled at how Jerry was holding up, and wondered what he would ever do if he lost Michelle. Mostly he didn't want to think about it, so he was happy to help change the subject. "Okay, why did you call?" he asked.

Derek got right to the point. "Jerry's story was pretty remarkable, quite a testimony, I think you call it. And I think it's courageous for him to share it with me, a stranger. But I'm not sure what it has to do with my situation. I mean,

I'm worried about my relationship with my wife and he's a widower. I'm concerned about my performance on the job — which for me means being out on the road. But he sits behind a desk all day analyzing survey data and setting up focus groups. So although I was impressed, I really don't see the connection."

"You're an observant fella," Tom said with a smile. "We are not going to slip anything past you. You're right. In a lot of ways Jerry's situation is very different from your own, so it might be hard to see the relevance in it to you. But let me ask you one question: What stood out in Jerry's story?"

Derek wasn't ready for that question. But he had been replaying Jerry's words in his head almost constantly since they met. He hesitated for a moment to collect his thoughts and then replied, "I think the substance of what he told me was that he encountered the power of faith, most of all in Sandy, but also in the members of her congregation. That power surprised him and moved him — and now it is helping him cope with his tragic loss. Without faith, I think he was telling me, nothing would make any sense. So he is grateful he was given the gift of faith before he lost the love of his life. How's that?"

"Better than I could do," Tom replied. "You really are a quick study, aren't you?"

Derek was happy to take the compliment and run with it, even if the run wasn't going to be very far. "It's a dirty world out there, and that's how I survive," he said. "And I do okay, if I must say so myself. Or at least I did. Like I told you, lately old Derek isn't bringing in the big bucks like he used to, and that's a strain in a couple of ways. What do you have in your bag of tricks to treat that?"

Tom chuckled at Derek's light-hearted appeal. "Well, I'm fresh out of printing presses to let you print your own money, so we're going to have to put on our thinking caps," he replied. "That means I'm going to have to ask another question. If you could do one thing to change your life around for the better, what would it be?"

Derek wasn't ready for this question either. But instead of offering a glib answer he decided to give it some serious thought. After a minute he wasn't sure. "You're asking me about changing just one thing, is that right?" he asked. Tom nodded, but sensing that Derek was ready to get started, he didn't say anything. "Well, it's hard to say just one thing, because I think it's a pattern, really. Over the years, especially when our children were small, Sally didn't have a lot of time for me. Oops, that's not politically correct. And it's not really fair either. Let me put it this way: Sally and I didn't have a lot of time for each other. After work I wanted to unwind. But home was a madhouse, and Sally always wanted either some adult company after a day with the kids or she wanted to get away, even just to go to the grocery store. Neither had much appeal to me, so I got in the habit of stopping with the guys after work and unwinding with them."

Derek's eyes took a longer focus. "That was a great release. We could trade war stories. We could cry in our beer over our disappointments and curse the darkness until our problems and frustrations didn't eat away at our insides. And you know what else? As we got closer we could brag about our successes and really celebrate them together. We got to be like brothers."

"I'll bet Sandy was thrilled for you," Tom teased.

"You know, it wasn't as bad as you might think," Derek replied. "I mean, I never had a firm quitting time, so she never expected me home at a particular time unless the kids had something to do. And I was always home on time for that. Every now and then the party would run a little late or I'd have a couple more drinks than usual and then she wasn't happy with me. But most of the time, it was just part of my day. I would just have a couple of drinks and it wasn't a problem at home. I didn't take any of my work home with me, and I told myself that was a noble thing to do. But now I can see that I was missing a lot not being at home, and my family was missing some big parts of me."

"So you dropped out of the group and now you're a world famous homebody?" Tom asked, trying to move the conversation along but keep it light.

"Not exactly," Derek laughed. "Fact is, those guys are my salvation, so to speak. I look to them for emotional support. I can't drink like I once could, and I don't want to, not with the crackdown on drinking and driving. But the group still gets together most nights, and I join them a few times a week if I'm not on the road. Over the years we started spending time in other ways too. Some of us like to hunt, so we take some hunting trips. Some of us like to fish so we take some fishing trips. Most of us like to golf, so that's always available. In fact, we joke that even though there are about a dozen of us in the big group, we always come down to three guys looking for a foursome. Between us we've got season tickets to the local pro football, basketball and hockey games, and one of the guys works for a company that has a skybox for baseball. So there's always something going on, always something to do."

"Sounds like a fun bunch of guys," Tom interjected, wondering if Derek had anything to say about the downside of things.

"It is!" said Derek, with a wry smile. "And that's the problem. There's always something to do, and I like doing things with them because we've grown so close emotionally over the years. Meanwhile, Sally and I just sort of vegetated. I did what I had to as a father and husband. But more and more my heart was with the guys. And as my circumstances improved, I spent more time with them."

"And your problem is?" Tom asked. He knew what the problem was, but he also knew Derek had to say it himself, in his own words — and hear himself say it.

"My problem is that the kids are getting older. That's a mixed blessing. I'll never miss diapers. But the challenges change. When they're around the house Sally wonders why I don't do more with them — take them golfing or fishing or hunting — instead of running off with my buddies. And when they're gone with friends, I think she resents being left alone."

"Sounds like you're coming into a major squeeze," Tom said.

"Good image," said Derek. "I do feel this squeeze. From a financial point of view, even with my recent setbacks I can afford to spend more time with my friends and I'd like to do that. But from the point of view of time, I have less time for that if I want to be a good husband and father — or even if I just want to do my duty and keep peace in the valley. So I'm torn. And I find that no matter what I'm doing, I'm not enjoying it much because I'm thinking I could or should be doing something else. It's like I'm always distracted, always conflicted, when I could be having fun — which, as you know, I like to do."

"Hey, everybody likes to have fun," Tom offered, hoping to keep Derek at ease so he would continue to speak freely.

"Listen, does this faith thing you're pushing offer a way for me to get past all this agonizing and just have more fun?" Derek asked. His tone was almost mocking, but Tom didn't take offense. Instead he asked a question.

"If I told you it did, would you believe me?" Tom asked.

"I don't know," Derek replied. "No offense, but I have to admit that I find it hard to use *church* and *fun* in the same sentence."

"I thought so," said Tom, laughing. "But you do have an open mind, don't you?"

"My wife says I have a blank mind," said Derek, joining in the laughter. "So what do you suggest?"

"I suggest you spend some time with Mary in human resources," Tom replied."

"Are you, the big Christian, trying to set me up with another woman?" Derek joked.

"Guilty!" Tom said with a chuckle. "Only behave yourself. Mary is old enough to be your mother and tough enough to whip your father. Here's her number," he said, jotting it down on a small piece of paper. Give her a call when it's convenient and tell her I asked you to call. I think she'll be happy to see you. And if you behave, I think she'll be willing to let you go without a bruise."

"Sounds like a real treat. I can't wait," said Derek, taking the piece of paper. "And seriously, Tom, thanks for your time." "No problem," said Tom. "My time's not really mine anyway."

Derek was heading out the door but Tom's comment stopped him. He turned with a quizzical look on his face. But before he could ask anything Tom added, "We'll save that for another time. It's closing, and this accountant is going to obey the clock."

Derek waved and headed down the hall.

A CLOSE ENCOUNTER

Derek had to take part in a sales convention at the end of the week, so he didn't have a chance to call Mary in human resources until the next Monday. He considered dropping the whole thing, but Tom's description of Mary intrigued him. He wasn't attracted to older women — certainly not those "old enough to be his mother." But now he found himself a little relieved that if he had to see a woman, she would be much older and probably not very attractive to him.

On his trip he had found himself in the hotel lounge sitting with a group of associates that included an attractive woman about 10 years younger than he was. She was not a stunning beauty, but a wholesome one, and her smile could have melted the polar ice cap. She was incredibly shy, and at first he spoke to her because he just wanted to put her at ease. But as the rounds came and went, the group dwindled down to just the two of them. By then she appeared very impressed by his achievements, which he was only too happy to share, and when the bartender said it was time for last call, he swallowed hard and asked her if she wanted to come up to his room for a nightcap from the mini-bar. Now he remembered her words like she was there, sitting across the table from him again. "I'd like that. I think I'd like that very much. But I promised my boyfriend I'd call him by 10, and he's out on the West Coast. So I better call it a night. But this was fun, and if you're around at closing time tomorrow night, I'll take you up on that offer of a nightcap. I think it could be very special." As she finished speaking, she rose from the table, leaned over and gave Derek a soft kiss on a cheek. "Thanks, she whispered. "You make me feel real special. Until tomorrow."

He was smitten. In fact, he didn't think much about anything else except his charm and her sweetness until the next morning, after he rose early as usual and made a pot of coffee in the little coffee maker beside his sink. Then something started to gnaw at him. The young woman hadn't really declined his offer. She had just *deferred* it. She had gone up to her room that night to presumably whisper sweet nothings in her boyfriend's ear — and that's all it would be, sweet words meaning nothing. What could they mean when she was looking forward to meeting another man the very next night and going up to his room for a "nightcap"? He had never thought of himself as "the other man" before. But now the thought of her duplicitous behavior bothered him. He poured another cup of coffee and decided to call room service for breakfast rather than go down to the hotel's coffee shop. She might be there, and although he had to admit that he was attracted to her and the prospect of spending more time with her, he did not want to see her again just now.

As it turned out, he did not see her again that night either. Before he had finished that first cup of coffee in his room, the office had called to say a client was trying to reach him and had left a number to call him early at home. Derek followed up right away and was happy — *relieved* — to hear that the client wanted to meet with him immediately to go over several complicated matters related to a pending sale.

He agreed to drive over, across the state, and be at the client's plant by 2 p.m. That impressed the client, which was good. And it got him out of what was bound to be a bad situation no matter how it turned out. As he waited for breakfast and packed his bag, he was pleased with himself and his good fortune.

He decided not to call the girl's room. No point in giving a late night whim more weight than it might deserve. No point in embarrassing the young woman if she was also having second thoughts. But he couldn't just disappear either. He could have called any number of people at the convention and explained his sudden departure. But he decided to call the room of a guy who worked with the young woman and would be sure to tell her. Derek explained that he was sorry he had to leave the convention early, but he needed to put out a fire at an important client's plant right away. "Give my best to everyone and tell them all I'm sorry I can't stick around and enjoy their company some more," he said, careful to keep his sentiments universal and his tone ever so casual. He was happy to let the opportunity for a nightcap slip away. But he couldn't take any pride in that because he had to admit that he was trying very hard to keep a door open too.

The incident crossed his mind as he prepared to dial Mary's number. He had come on to women before, it's true. But he told himself that those were innocent flirtations. After all, he had never followed through. And even if a woman had been as favorably disposed as the woman was at the convention, it wasn't clear that he would have been unfaithful to Sally. In fact, when he finally did get a green light, hadn't he packed up and escaped temptation? That should count for *something,* shouldn't it? He wasn't sure of any of this as Mary's phone started to ring. He was just grateful that she was older — "much older" is the way Tom had put it.

She answered cheerfully, introducing herself by her name and asking how she could be of service. "Hello, I'm Derek, I'm a friend of Tom's from the sales department, and he suggested that I get in touch with you." Derek didn't think he would have to explain much because he assumed that Tom had already contacted Mary just as he had called Jerry. But Mary didn't seem to have a clue. "I don't know a Tom in the sales department," she said.

"I'm sorry," Derek interjected. "I should have been clearer. I'm the one in the sales department. The Tom who told me to call you is in accounting."

Mary's tone changed immediately. "Oh yes, that Tom. I should have guessed. He's always sending people to me. What can I do for you — you said it was Derek, right?"

"Yes, that's right. But didn't Tom call you and mention that he had referred me to you?" Derek asked, still a little surprised.

"No, but don't worry. He never does," Mary said. Her tone was chatty and almost motherly. "My office is always open and I'm always happy to see a friend of Tom's." She paused for a second. "You did want to see me, is that right?" she said.

"Yes, and I still do," Derek said, always eager to have fun with the use of language.

"Well, good," Mary replied "When *do* you want to meet?"

Derek didn't want to sound too familiar, so he didn't suggest lunch. "How about first thing after lunch, say 1:30?" he asked.

"Too cheap to buy lunch, are you? Did you say you were Tom's friend or his brother?" she asked. Derek caught the humor and appreciated it. Before he could reply with a crack of his own, Mary added: "Okay, 1:30 then. I'll mark you down as Derek the Cheapskate for 1:30."

By now Derek had a chance to collect himself. "How about Derek the Generous for lunch at 11:45? Can you handle that?" he asked. His pride was worth more than the price of a lunch.

"I can," Mary replied. "Derek the Generous for lunch at 11:45. I'll meet you down in the corridor on first floor. I'll look for a guy with a fat wallet because you'll need one if you want to take me to lunch."

"I've got the fattest wallet in town," Derek answered. "But to avoid hassles I keep it under a gray topcoat. Look for the handsome specimen of manly salesmanship with the gray topcoat and shoes with a good shine on them," he offered.

"See you then," said Mary. "I'm looking forward to it."

Derek hung up his phone, pleased that he'd held his own but admitting that Mary seemed to have a personality that matched Tom's description of her.

MARY'S STORY

Derek arrived in the lobby right at 11:45 and saw an older woman in a gray suit looking out the window next to the door. But he couldn't be sure if that was Mary so he decided not to approach her. In a few seconds she turned, noticed him, smiled and walked directly over to him. "You must be Derek," she said, her smile growing broader as she reached out her hand to him.

He was struck by the air of assurance she had. It was apparent in her walk, her posture, her greeting and her tone of voice. "Yes, I'm Derek," he said, smiling and shaking her out- stretched hand. "And you must be Mary."

"You've got it," she said, suddenly a little less refined. "And since you made the date, I get to pick the place. You've got that fat wallet with you, right?" she asked. One phrase came to Derek's mind immediately. *Down to earth.* Mary was assured and down to earth — very down to earth. He didn't always like that in a woman, but he found that with Mary it made him feel very relaxed and at ease. He decided there was enough difference in their age that he could tease her a bit too without giving offense. "You better be worth it," he said in as firm a tone as he could muster.

Mary was not one to back off. "I am, buster, you can bet on it," she said. Derek liked her smile and the sparkle in her eye. "So where are we going, Mary?" he asked.

"Follow me, she said," obviously comfortable with the lead. They walked out the door and down the street a few blocks to a simple little café, making small talk along the way. Inside they hung their coats on hooks and seated themselves in a booth. Derek had looked to help Mary with her coat and hang it up for her, but she was ahead of him at every move. She even led him to the booth.

"I had no idea we were going to a place so elegant," Derek said with feigned awe. "Do you think one fat wallet will be enough here?"

"Not if you leave it out where Tony can get it," Mary said as an elderly man in shirtsleeves approached their table. "Derek, this is Tony, of whom I was just speaking so highly. Tony, meet Derek. And Derek, don't shake hands. When Tony's around you want to keep both hands in your pockets."

Of course it was too late for that. Derek and Tony were already shaking hands. "Thanks, Mary, that's the nicest thing you've said to me in years," Tony said. Then he turned to Derek and spoke in a stage whisper, "I've been convicted of murder and my sentencing hearing is next week. I could get the chair. Mary's my only character witness. Do you have any suggestions?"

"Don't pay the electric bill," Derek offered.

Tony laughed out loud. So did Mary. Derek was pretty pleased with himself. Tony looked Mary in the eye. "I should have known, birds of a feather flock together," he said. Then looking at Derek again, he said, "Enjoy your lunch. I'm responsible for the food but not for the company. *Bon apetit.*"

"You two sure have quite a rapport," Derek said.

"We should," Mary replied. "When he's not rustling cattle or swindling old widows, he's my brother," Mary explained.

"The best thing I'll say about the food is that he gives me a good discount. But you, you're going to have to pay full price," she added, still smiling.

"And it's a bargain at any price," Derek said, making a grandiose sweeping motion, "if what you have to tell me helps me continue my journey."

"And what do I have to tell you?" asked Mary, looking very confused.

"You don't know?" Derek replied. "I thought Tom referred me to you because you have something to say, a story to tell that can help me with some things going on in my life right now." He decided to lighten the tone just a bit. "Hey, this isn't a setup, is it? Tony isn't cutting you and Tom in on a share of luncheon proceeds, is he?"

"Of course he is. Otherwise no one would eat here," Mary joked. "Seriously, I do have a story to tell. In fact, I've got a lot of stories to tell. If I told them all, you'd be feeding me for years. But if Tom told you to find me, I think I know what story he has in mind."

"You do? Simple as that?" Derek asked, a little surprised that Mary could assume so much with so little to go on.

"Look, Tom and I have known each other since Tom was wet behind the ears. We've shared a lot. And we still do, as a matter of fact. Since neither of us has to travel much for the company, we're among the most regular attendees at the Wednesday noon prayer and Bible study meetings. We've been doing it for almost 10 years now. So when he sends someone to meet with me who says he or she is going through some personal turmoil and expects to hear a story, I know what's expected of me."

Derek liked the word "turmoil." It had a much better ring than "problems," because often he wondered if the "problems" he thought he was having weren't just little things he was magnifying in his own mind. But certainly he was going through personal turmoil. So that was a good term and he wanted to tell Mary that. But first he had to deal with that other phrase she used: "expected of me."

So he asked her, "Did you use the term *expected of me?* I'm sorry, I don't want to give any offense, but that makes it sound like you're a paid performer."

Mary laughed. "No, I'm not a paid performer. At least not any more. What I meant to say was that I know what it is that other people in my circle of faith friends are *relying* on me to do — or in this instance, to convey to you. After all, I do feel a sense of responsibility toward them or I wouldn't be here, having lunch with a man who is a perfect stranger to me."

"Okay, I get your point," said Derek. "No offense intended. I would like to hear your story."

"None taken — and I appreciate the opportunity to share it with you, Derek. Why don't we order and I'll get started? It'll take a while to get our food. As I like to tell Tony, his motto should be, 'If you think our food is bad, you haven't tried our service.' That usually gets a rise out of him."

While they waited for the waitress, Mary offered some ground rules. "Derek, I'm going to ask you to be discreet. My story is not confidential, but neither do I broadcast it all over town. If Tom thinks you should hear it, I am happy to tell it to you. But it's not a pretty story in many respects, and

I ask that you not share it with others at our workplace."
Derek was intrigued, but he quickly agreed. Mary started to
tell her story.

"Do you know what I am, Derek?" she asked.

"If Tom told me to see you, I guess you must be a
Christian, right?" he answered, not at all sure where Mary
was heading with her question.

"Okay, fair enough, I'm a Christian. But do you know
what I was before that? Do you know what I *am* before that,
even today?" Before Derek could respond, Mary continued,
"I'm a sinner, Derek. You hear that? I'm a sinner. Always was.
Guess I always will be, too, as long as I draw breath —
though I really wish that wasn't the case. But let's start with
that reality. I'm a sinner right now, as we sit here. That's
where my story begins, Derek. That's where everything
begins for me — with acceptance of the reality that no
matter what, I'm a sinner."

Derek was uneasy with the conversation, but he felt he
had to say something. "Okay, you're a sinner. But isn't
everybody? I think I remember learning that in Sunday
school. Everybody is a sinner and Christ came to save
them."

"*Them,* Derek?" Mary asked. "Okay, let's let that slip by
for now. You remember your Sunday school lesson pretty
well. It's true that Christianity teaches that everybody is a
sinner. But I'm not talking about everybody just now. I'm
not talking about you, or Tony, or Tom. I'm talking about *me,*
Derek. And I'm telling you and I'm telling God that I'm a
sinner. My faith journey begins with that sad, sorrowful,
pathetic fact. Some people aren't comfortable with that

notion. They like to focus on how we are saved. And by the way, I believe that too. But being saved wouldn't mean much to me if I didn't know what I was being saved from. And what I am being saved from is not just my sins, but my *sinfulness.*"

Derek was still uncomfortable with Mary's words, but even more uncomfortable with the silence that followed. But he didn't know what to say, so he chose a basic question. "And that's important, right?" he asked, not at all sure of what he was doing.

"Yes, for me it is a supremely important first step. First, I had to acknowledge my sinfulness. And then, confronted by that awful truth, I had to deal with another truth. But fortunately, this truth is a magnificent one. God loves me. God loves me in my sinfulness. He loved me so much He sent his only son to suffer and die for my sins. His love is unconditional. God loves me no matter what — no matter who I am, no matter what I do. For me the most amazing part is that God loves me even when I don't love myself — even when I *can't* love myself. Knowing that, Derek, I am so full of love that I want to respond in love. I want to do and to be my very best."

"That's it? That's how *you* achieve excellence?" he asked, a little relieved that the topic had moved to pleasant things like love and away from sin, a concept that made him uncomfortable.

"No, Derek, that's not it. That's not *it* at all. I am not talking about me achieving anything on my own. But I don't expect you to get it immediately. If you don't mind a baseball metaphor, we're still in the first inning. But don't worry, we have plenty of time because the service is worse than the food." She was smiling, but she wasn't slowing down.

"As I was saying, knowledge of God's unconditional love for me motivates me to respond in kind. I want to love Him. I want to do His will. But remember what I said at the start: I'm a sinner. So what happens when I try to live up to God's love for me? Sometimes I succeed. I do good things. But sometimes I fail. And some of those times, my failures are memorable. In fact, some have been, at least at one level, truly and permanently life-changing. But at another level, there is always hope. Hope in a God who saves. So I regret my sins. Words cannot convey how deeply I regret some of them. But I don't despair of my sins. Or of my sinfulness. I believe that God wants the very best for me — now and for all eternity. So I have hope. I keep trying. And I've come to see that by His grace I can do better. I can turn my life around and make my life more closely resemble what I want it to be, which is a tribute to His love and concern for the world. I know I have a long way to go, Derek. But I'm grateful now for where I am. And I'm grateful for the little signposts along the way that tell me from time to time that I'm on the right track."

"Signposts?" Derek asked. He was confused.

"I think God gives me some little signs from time to time that tell me I'm heading in the right direction and encourage me to keep trying. But let's not get sidetracked by that just yet. Let's talk about the key concepts here. Sinfulness. Infinite and unconditional love — a love for us greater than we have for ourselves. And grace — think of it as God's vitamin supplement that lets us be better than we could on our own, if we didn't have His nourishment.

Finally, there's community, Derek. My Christian community. It's a gift from God. Without it, I could put the pieces together but I couldn't keep them together. For me, those concepts cover a lot of what I have come to consider the core of Christian faith. I'm no theologian and I probably wouldn't even make much of a preacher, but I do what I can with what I've got."

Derek had the sense that he wasn't keeping up, but he was intrigued by what he heard. "I think you would make a fine preacher," he said. "But I won't comment on your potential as a theologian, because I don't even know what that is."

They both laughed.

"Anyway, it's not so bad for a whore, wouldn't you say?" Mary asked.

Derek spit his soup back into the bowl. "A what?" he asked incredulously. He was not sure if he had ever heard a woman use that word, and he was absolutely sure he had never heard a woman use it to describe herself.

"A whore," Mary repeated. Her words were completely incongruous with the sweet, almost angelic smile that shone from her face. "I'm a whore. Or at least I was a whore." Derek hadn't moved. He continued to lean over his soup, his spoon in his hand, his mouth open in shock. Mary could see that he couldn't speak, so she continued.

"I wasn't a street walker. But I was a prostitute in that I provided a man sex for services. I slept my way to the top, Derek. It happened on my first job after I graduated from an executive secretary program at a local business college. I was 20. My boss was just 30, moving into a junior executive post and getting his own secretary for the first time. But you could tell he was on the fast track, heading to the top. He was so dashing, so charismatic. I remember after our interview I met a friend and told her, "I wish I was rich so I would work for him for nothing. I'd do *anything* to be his secretary. And the sad thing is, Derek, in the end I did.

"He hired me, and I came on board with starry eyes. I worked hard because I was in awe of him, and I did good work. The first time he asked me if I wanted to stop for a drink with him after work, I could barely respond without losing all my composure. Of course, I went. It wasn't awkward. He was a perfect gentleman. After my second drink, he took my hand which was resting on the table and held it and said, 'Mary, you are the most awesome secretary anyone could have. I just wanted to thank you for all the good work you do.' It was a simple gesture, and I found myself wishing it were more. We started to go out like that, for just an hour after work, regularly on Wednesdays for about six months.

"Then he had to go on a trip. It was a big meeting with an important vendor and he was going to be negotiating a lot of complex details and signing several contracts before he came home. So he asked me to go along. I was ecstatic. To make a long story short, it was like a honeymoon — only we weren't married. We had what I thought was a wonderful week, and what he said to me on the way home made me feel so very close to him. So the affair continued. In fact, it continued for 20 years. When he started his own business, I moved with him and he made me his first assistant. He always touted the quality of my work in public and with his family members, and he had incredible control so we never let on in the office when anyone else was around. He made sure we always had a compelling work-related reason to spend time together, and he sold that to everyone — except a few very close friends, as I learned later.

"Apart from them, he kept our relationship a secret until one weekend when we were in the office together and his wife happened to stop by and walk in on a delicate scene. I felt like a tramp. She stormed out. But after a few moments, he regained his supremely self-confident air and assured me everything would be okay. For once he was wrong. Nothing was okay after that. Of course, now I can see that nothing had been okay from the first day I saw him. Back then I wanted to believe him. But I learned quickly and painfully that it was not going to be the same again, ever. At times he had indicated that he would someday leave his wife for me. I held out hope all those years. But soon enough it was clear that he was going to stay with her and I had to find a new job — a new *life,* really."

Derek was engrossed in Mary's story. When she paused, he was quick with a question. "What did you do?"

"I came apart, Derek. As I have put it with some people, I slept my way to the top and I drank my way to the bottom. I was devastated. Suddenly, I had no job. I had lost my closest friend and consort. Apart from the emotional pain, I had a lot of free time on my hands. So I sunk like a rock, Derek. There's a whole year of my life that's pretty hazy. Then, fortunately, an old friend took an interest in me and started to slowly help me work my way back to health. Part of the problem was that I had a lot of reasons to dislike myself. I had let my relationship with that man define me and define my life. I didn't have a support network to help me because

I hadn't built one. My family is small and spread all over the country. And I was embarrassed by the whole affair, so I didn't want to tell any of them about it.

"I didn't know what to do, where to go, who to reach out to. But I couldn't sit in my apartment and mope. I'd have a drink or two, then decide I didn't want to drink alone, and so I'd go to a little lounge just down the street and spend the day there, trying to visit with whomever I could until I could barely talk. Then someone would suggest I go home. Sometimes I didn't go home alone, and sometimes I didn't go to my place. But usually I'd stagger back to my place alone and fall asleep on my couch. It had become a real pattern until an old friend from my high school days called — out of the blue, I thought then — and asked me to go to lunch. I poured my heart out to her and she got me some help. I didn't want to cooperate at first, but she kept coming around and gradually convinced me to attend Alcoholics Anonymous with her. Turns out she had developed a problem while her husband was busy traveling and building his business, so I wasn't walking that path alone. It was a long, slow process, and I confess I slipped more than once. But today, by the grace of God and the friends He has sent me, I've been dry for eight years."

She lifted her coffee cup as if to make a toast and Derek found himself lifting his to softly clink against hers. "Congratulations," he said, relieved that the story had a brighter side.

"The thing is, Derek, it's a painful process to confront the demons inside — especially if you've been feeding them all your adult life. But it's an even bigger struggle to fill the voids.

For me the voids were huge. The one that's been hardest for me is that I don't have any children. When I wallowed in my self-pity, I could blame *him*. But gradually I came to see that I have to take responsibility for it. It's part of the life I chose. It wasn't a conscious decision. But it flowed as a natural consequence of decisions I did make. It's an unspeakable loss, and it's difficult for me to face up to the fact that it was my choice, my responsibility.

"In fact, I couldn't face up to it without my fellow church members. They have helped me fill the voids and find new reasons to live — and the funny thing is, most of them don't even know it. They just know me as a middle-age single woman with a lot of energy who likes to do a lot of volunteer work. Sometimes they'll ask me if I'm widowed or if I ever married, and I say, 'No, I just didn't find the right man.' And that's the truth. I found a man, but he was definitely not the right one for me to settle down with and build a life together. So now I'm building a new life, a little late in life — but I'm definitely not doing it alone!

"By the grace of God, I have my faith community, and it has helped me beyond words fill the voids that my friends in AA helped me see I was trying to fill with alcohol. So Derek, ultimately my story is a story of redemption, but it's also a story of community. By God's grace two communities saved me and those communities now help keep me on track, giving me the context in which to have a meaningful life."

"That's a fascinating story," Derek said with genuine sincerity. "But I'm a little confused. I wonder why Tom had you tell it to me. I mean, your circumstances are so different from mine."

It was Mary's turn to be curious. "How are they different, Derek?"

"Well, I don't want to sound like a Goody-Two Shoes or holier-than-thou," Derek said, "but we're different in almost every way possible, Mary. I'm a male, married, I've got kids, I've never had an affair, and I'm not an alcoholic."

"Maybe Tom was trying to give to you what I call the boot camp shock treatment," Mary replied. "The what?" Tom asked in earnest.

"I call it the boot camp shock treatment. You know, when you go to boot camp, you step off the bus and you step into a new universe. Everything is different. Maybe Tom wanted you to see what it's like on the other side. My guess is that you told him that you've thought about having affairs, maybe even drifted in that direction a time or two, and that you also indicated that you spend quite a bit of time with your hand around a beverage — wondering if it's time to step across the line. In my life I have lived two existences. Maybe Tom wanted you to get a safe, second-hand taste of what life would be like on the other side if you give in and do the easy thing."

"Maybe," Derek agreed, still not entirely convinced.

"And maybe Tom just wanted you to hear how important a faith community is to keeping one's life on track," Mary added. "I mean, if faith communities could bring me back from the brink and help me find a life with meaning and purpose — despite the very poor decisions I made that have had dreadful lifelong consequences and despite my chemical dependency — maybe he hoped that you would see how a faith community could help you. Maybe you're the one who has to connect the dots."

"I think you're right," Derek replied, finally persuaded. Just then the waitress arrived with their food. By now Derek was famished, and he dug into his plate like a dog in a butcher shop. Suddenly he was conscious of how fast he was eating. "Sorry," he said, looking up and trying to speak clearly with a little food still in his mouth.

Mary smiled. "No problem. Like I told you, the only thing worse than the food is the service. And the service is so bad, by the time you get your food, you're happy to eat anything. I tell Tony that's the secret to his success."

Derek laughed and nodded. "Obviously you're doing well with our company," he said, trying to change the conversation's focus and let things end on a pleasant note.

Mary put down her fork. "Not all my decisions were bad. And sometimes God seems to look out for us in spite of ourselves. While I worked for my paramour, I took advantage of company programs to finish my undergraduate degree. When he started his own company and I followed him, he encouraged me to pursue an MBA in night classes and his company paid my tuition. At the time I saw it mostly as a way to help fill the many evenings between his visits. He encouraged me, probably for the wrong reasons. It gave him a night that I didn't expect him to spend with me. And he knew I would put my schoolwork first, so there was less time to cultivate the sort of healthy social relationships that someone like me should have had.

"In any event," she continued, "after his wife discovered us, gave him an ultimatum and he said I had to go, at least I had a few things going for me. I didn't see them at first. As I said, I sunk like a rock in the ocean. But when others found me, encouraged me to come up to the top for air, and then helped me find my way, at least I had some credentials to use as building blocks in my new life. I was able to find a job that pays well, is satisfying, gives me enough freedom to pursue my volunteer opportunities, and makes it relatively easy to feel good about myself at the end of the day. But don't get me wrong, the threads that tie it all together for me now are my faith and my faith-communities. I don't miss my AA meetings and I don't miss my church meetings — because if I do, I am convinced, I will lose my way immediately. They truly are my *lifelines.*"

Derek had never heard faith communities described like that, and he certainly hadn't experienced them in that way when he was a child and accompanied his parents to church. So he was skeptical. Yet, he was impressed with Mary — with how far she had sunk and how together her life seemed to be at the moment, despite some deep sorrows and some obviously painful losses. He had one more question on the way back to the office. "Mary, are you saying that if you had your life to live over again, you would do it differently?"

Mary, who was walking to his right, slowed almost to a stop, so Derek had to slow down and turn to avoid losing contact. When he did, he found himself looking into Mary's eyes. "Yes, Derek, that's what I'm saying. If I had my life to live over again, I would do it very differently. Why? Because I am a sinner who is sorry for her sins. I wish I had not done many of the things I have done. But you know something else, Derek? I don't think about that very much because I don't have my life to live over. All I have is this life. It's the one God gave to me, and it's the one I have to live. In the final analysis I'm grateful for it.

"So I deeply regret some decisions I've made in life, but I don't regret my life. And I've decided that my calling — my vocation — is to live the life I have been given as well as I can live it, one day at a time. I know I will make mistakes, that I will falter, and when I do I pray for the strength to say I am sorry to whomever I've wronged. I pray for the resolve to try even harder in the future, and I pray for the grace to achieve that improvement. Let me put it this way, Derek, I've got regrets but my regrets don't have me."

Derek decided that Mary offered a lot of food for thought, and he should think about it some more later when he had some time alone. For the moment, he had one more question. "Mary," he said, "I can't tell you how grateful I am for your willingness to share your story with me. But one thing confuses me. You described both your church and your AA group as faith-based communities. I thought AA was a secular organization. Am I wrong about that?"

"Not entirely," Mary chuckled. "In one sense, it is secular because it requires no belief of any kind on the part of its members, and it's only purpose is to help people obtain sobriety. However, AA's founders developed 12 steps on the path to sobriety, and they are our cornerstones to recovering. God is mentioned several times in those steps — and not just in a peripheral way. In the first step, AA's founders admitted that they were powerless over alcohol. In the second, they expressed belief that there is a Power greater than themselves that could restore them to sanity. In the third step, they made a decision to turn their wills and their lives "over to the care of God" as they understood Him. In steps five, six and 11, God also is clearly integral to the process. And step 12 talks about a "spiritual awakening" that they experienced as a result of taking the first 11 steps. So AA is a religious community in the sense that it recognizes that there is some Power beyond us, and without it we cannot be saved."

Derek liked to say he "enjoyed a drink as much anyone," but he had never been concerned that he was an alcoholic. So although he had heard about AA and knew its purpose, he had never heard any of the things Mary was telling him. He found it intriguing that people who were truly dependent on a chemical substance — physically and well as psychologically — could overcome its destructive influence on their lives by resorting to a "higher power" that was religious in nature. "So you're saying that AA affirms your belief in God?" he asked.

"Yes, that's true. But I'm saying a lot more than that, Derek. I'm saying that AA was the first place where I came face to face with God's healing power, and my church community was the second place where that happened. I'm also saying that it is in these communities that I experience God's love for me and His healing power working in me. To sum it up, Derek, what I'm saying is that I cannot imagine having access to God's love and healing apart from my faith communities. Just as I can't stay sober myself, I couldn't find a meaningful, purposeful life by myself. I need God to provide those things, and in my experience He always provides them in the context of a community.

"Let me be clear about this. God doesn't need the community to save you. But *you* need the community to experience His saving power and grace. I know that goes against a lot of what passes for religious faith today. You know, 'just me and Jesus' — I go through life practicing the Golden Rule and Jesus is up there smiling at how good I'm doing. I know that view is popular, Derek, but it just doesn't cut it for me. And you know what else? That doesn't cut it for the millions who have been helped and are still being helped by AA. That doesn't cut it for the many millions more who go to church each Sunday. In fact, I was pleased to find that many of the support groups at our church use variations of AA's 12-step program, and I'm helping to adapt it to some of the areas where I do volunteer service."

They were coming to the front door of their office building as Mary finished speaking. As he opened the door for her, their bubble of privacy burst. There were several people in the corridor. "Thanks for the lunch and the advice," Derek said softly.

"You're most welcome," Mary replied, in a very business-like tone. "I hope I've given you a lot of food for thought. If you have more questions, feel free to contact me. Oh, and I almost forgot, Tom said he hopes you get back to him too."

Derek smiled. Anyone overhearing them would have to conclude that their lunch was *all* business. Bringing in another man's name at the end was the perfect thing to do. "Mary is bright," Derek thought as he waved and turned toward the elevators, away from the direction of Mary's office. He was still mulling over everything she had told him about herself when his phone rang. "Hey, it's Tom, how did your lunch go, Derek?" his friend was asking.

"I'm not sure I can put it into words yet, Tom. But she sure has a story to tell. In fact, that's all I've been thinking about since I got back to my desk. I better change gears quickly or I won't be prepared for my trip tomorrow."

"Well, I won't keep you then, Derek," Tom replied. "But if you want to meet again and maybe make contact with some other friends I have around here, just let me know. I'm available for you anytime."

"Thanks, Tom," Derek replied. "I really appreciate it. How about next Wednesday, the day after I get back? I've got to come up there and drop off my expense report anyway."

"I'll see you then. Have a good trip," Tom said just before hanging up. Derek was able to put his conversation with Mary in the back of his mind while he finished preparations for his sales trip. But as soon as he had everything he needed and left the office to head home, he found his attention drifting back to what Mary had told him at lunch. Coming through the door at home broke the spell. But as soon as he sat down on the plane the next morning and strapped himself in the seatbelt, he found himself transported again back to the conversation with Mary at the little diner. There were a few things he wanted to take up with Tom as soon as he got back into the office and could get upstairs with his expense report.

WHY ME?

Bright and early the next Wednesday morning, Tom was at his desk "counting beans" when he noticed Derek getting off the elevator. Derek dropped his expense report on the desk of the accounting department's receptionist and then looked up to see Tom smiling at him. He headed directly into Tom's office with a big smile of his own. "How ya doing? Got a few minutes?" he said as he stepped through the door. "Sure do," said Tom. He rose to shake Derek's hand and motioned him to take a seat as he stepped around his desk and took a chair next to Derek.

"So how was your sales trip?" Tom asked. "Fine," Derek replied. "I didn't get everything I had hoped for, but it went better than I feared it might." He was still smiling. "But that's not what I'm here to talk about," he continued. "That Mary in the human resources department is something else."

"You found her interesting?" Tom responded, hoping Derek would go on.

"Interesting? I'm not sure that word does her justice. Maybe *overwhelming* would be better," Derek replied. "She has quite a story to tell, and I was surprised by her candor. It's not a story you'd want to tell everyone."

"You're right," Tom said. "She doesn't tell everyone. She is willing to be witness for her faith when the circumstances call for it, but I'm sure she asked you to be discreet."

"Yes, she did," Derek responded. "And I'll certainly respect that. You know, I also respect her trust in you. She was willing to tell her story to me, a complete stranger, just because you referred me to her. She trusts you a lot, Tom, and that's quite a compliment."

"I do feel honored by that," Tom replied, "And there's nothing I would do to betray that trust. But I have to tell you, it's like that with many of the friends I have made in the Christian communities to which I belong."

"Communities? You mean you belong to more than one?" Derek asked, more than a little incredulously."

"Well, yes and no," said Tom, with a bit of tease in his tone. "I believe that ultimately there really is just one Christian community. St. Paul says we should think of ourselves as the body of Christ. But as I experience life, I have the experience of belonging to several Christian communities — in the sense that people in each of the groups generally don't interact with people in the other groups. From the perspective of our *experience,* I guess you could say I belong to at least three Christian communities."

"Okay," said Derek. "I'll bite. Tell me what they are."

"Glad to," said Tom, his smile growing larger. "First, I belong to my local church congregation, which is part of a larger church organization. It's through that affiliation that I participate in worship with my family and the larger faith community. There I also find opportunities to serve, which for me is a matter of *living* my faith, and also opportunities to learn, which amounts to *feeding* my faith. For me worship, service and growth are things that I value. They help keep me on track, so I cherish that affiliation with a large Christian community.

"Next there's the men's group I belong to, which is a smaller group that is sponsored by my congregation. That gives me an opportunity to interact with guys like myself. I like that because there I've met people with some of the same interests and hobbies and challenges that I have. Only now that I think about it, some are older and some are younger, some are wealthier and some don't have much. I guess we're really a pretty diverse lot. But we do have our faith in common, so we can pray together and work together on some worthwhile projects. Of the 35 of us who get together monthly, there are four or five whom I would consider friends, and we do things outside of the group meetings."

"Like what, pray some more?" Derek asked, obviously skeptical of how manly a Christian men's group could be.

"Well, we might do that, especially if we haven't seen any sign of deer when we're out hunting," Tom replied.

"You hunt and shoot God's creatures?" Derek asked, engaging in a little good-natured mocking.

Tom was ready for his question. "We hunt a lot, shoot less — and hit the target almost never," he said with a chuckle. "Seriously, I know hunting is a controversial thing in our society, and I'm not saying that it's a Christian activity. Let's leave that discussion for another day. All I'm saying is that my little circle does most of the same things any group of men might do — we hunt, we fish, we play some cards and we'll even have a drink or two while we're doing it. Of course, not everybody in the larger, formal men's group would be comfortable with all of those things. Like I said, we're a diverse group.

"But I appreciate the opportunity to get together with other men in a wholesome environment to pray and talk about the challenges we experience at work and at home.

Then, of the 35 or so in that group, there is a handful of us who do more things together. Actually, when it comes to fishing, sometimes I also take out a couple of older guys in our big group who can't drive anymore. It started as a good deed, but I quickly discovered that they really know their business when it comes to fishing. One of them showed me a way to reel in a jig bait that makes it irresistible. And I'm convinced that's why I landed that big lunker last year on our annual north woods fishing jaunt."

"So you're saying it's a two-way street? You do some good and the old guys you help also help you?" asked Derek, himself an avid fisherman.

"Right. We're all better for having the experience of the group," Tom replied. "At one level our meetings remind me that I'm not alone, that there are other guys just like me who have dreams and hopes and fears and burdens — and who know that God is there somewhere in the mix of it all. At another level, it gives me an opportunity to meet good people, to do some good for some of them, and to let them do some good for me. At yet another level, I've made some deep and lasting friendships that I really cherish. I really can't begin to describe how true friends make life so much better. In a phrase, I'd say they make the good parts so much richer and the bad parts tolerable — and I don't have to tell you life brings us plenty of both."

"That's for sure," Derek was happy to interject. "Are there any more of these Christians communities you want to mention?"

"Just one, the one here at the company," Tom replied. "We meet as a group once a week. There are about a dozen of us. That's why we sometimes jokingly call ourselves *the apostles*. We meet for lunch at the café next door. The folks there reserve a room for us every Wednesday, and usually about eight or 10 of us are able to show up. It's different than the men's group because, as you know, the lunch bunch includes men and women. And we also come from different congregations and denominations. The two things we have in common is our work here and our Christian faith."

"So what do you do? Eat fishes and loaves?" asked Derek, reviving that tone of mild mocking he had used before.

"Oh sure, show off your knowledge of the scriptures," Tom responded. They both laughed. "Actually, we what we do is order our food, recite a brief prayer, read and discuss a short passage from the scriptures, and then we eat," Tom explained. "That's it, except we close with a prayer. People can share intentions or keep them private."

"Like if your boss is there and you want to pray that he or she gets fired?" Derek teased.

"You're not that far off," Tom said. "A few years ago one person did confide in me after lunch that her private intention was that her boss accept a new job offer halfway across the country. We all have our limits," he added with a chuckle.

"One more question," Derek interjected. "What if you haven't, as Mary so delicately put it, 'slept your way to the top and drank your way to the bottom'? What if you're just an ordinary schmo like me — not a bad guy really, but trying to do a little better with your life? Why would I want to join even one Christian community? I mean, I've already got a lot of good friends. In fact, I meet three of them pretty religiously every Sunday morning at the golf course. Why would I want to give that up? And what good would these Christian communities do for me, anyway?"

Tom sensed that Derek wasn't really interested in any answers to that question at the moment, and he didn't want to engage in a debate about the value of belonging to and participating in a Christian community. So he deflected the question with a suggestion. "Do you know Joe down in building maintenance?" he asked.

"You mean Joe the Schmo?" Derek asked with a smile?

"Well, some people called him that back in high school," Tom responded. "And when you asked why an ordinary schmo like yourself might want to be part of a Christian community, I thought of him. Why not go to the source?"

"Can a fine Christian guy like you call someone a schmo?" Derek asked, happy to be teasing again.

"He calls himself that," Tom replied. "He even gave a short presentation once at one of our luncheons called 'Why God Loves Schmos — a Biblical Survey.' It was hilarious, and instructive too. I'd say it was one of our best sessions. Why don't you give him a call and ask him about it? Tell him I suggested it."

"Okay. If it's half as good as the lunch I had with Mary, I'll treat you to a lunch after I meet Joe," said Derek, getting up to go. "Anyway, thanks for the time. I don't know why exactly, but I do enjoy visiting with you."

"The feeling is mutual," Tom responded. "I was really looking forward to you stopping by this morning, and I'm glad you did. And I'll be looking forward to seeing you again after you and Joe get together."

"Okay, it's a date then," Derek said as he headed for the elevator. For just a second Tom thought about calling Joe to give him a "heads-up" about Derek planning to contact him. But he decided that Joe would do just fine with a cold call from Derek. "I'll leave that in God's hands," he said to himself as he went back to his work. The big quarterly report to the board was due on his boss' desk at the end of the day.

JOE'S STORY

As Derek prepared to call Joe for an appointment, he was uneasy. He had known of Joe back in high school, but to his knowledge they had never spoken. Derek remembered Joe as a kid who had definitely come from the wrong side of the tracks. He was short and skinny, with narrow, deep-set eyes, and his clothes only added to his awkward appearance. Derek always assumed his family had "just gotten off the boat," as he and his friends had put it. Some of Derek's friends had made Joe the butt of jokes from time to time. But Derek had just ignored Joe, like he didn't exist. Derek hadn't mentioned any of this to Tom because Tom had been the kind of kid back in school who got along with everyone. He wouldn't understand. Derek was nervous about calling Joe, but he decided to go ahead with the plan because he had come to trust Tom and his judgment. If Tom said Joe was worth seeing, Derek would give it a try.

When he called, he was relieved to find out that Joe was not at his desk and he could just leave a voice-mail message. He was not sure how to approach Joe, so he was glad to put the ball in Joe's court and see what he did with it. Joe called him back about an hour later and instantly put him at ease. "This is Joe down in building maintenance. What can I do to make *your* day better, Derek?" he asked.

"Thanks for getting back to me so quickly," Derek said. "It's not an emergency, but Tom up in accounting suggested I get in touch with you. We were talking about the prayer group here, and he said you might be able to tell me more about the good things it does for its members."

"Well, I'm happy to hear that you weren't having a problem with anything in the building," said Joe with a chuckle. His tone sounded much more outgoing than Derek remembered Joe. "And I'd be even happier to tell you what the weekly group sessions do for me," he added. "How about over the lunch hour today?"

"Sure," Derek retorted, feeling himself on familiar turf. "I'll treat."

"No need to," said Joe. "I'm short-handed and I need to cover the phone over noon hour. So I brought a lunch to eat in my office. Just head across the street to the deli and get whatever suits you. I've got sodas down here, if that's what you want to drink. Does 12:10 work for you?"

"I'll be there," said Derek. He spent the rest of the morning working on a sales proposal. From time to time he glanced over at the clock on his desk that he had won for being the company's top salesman several years ago. Finally, at 11:50, he got up and headed to the deli across the street to be a little ahead of the crowd. Within a couple of minutes he was heading back across the street with a big submarine sandwich and some chips tucked under his arm. He took the elevator down to the ground floor and followed the signs to "building engineering." Finally, he stepped through a set of double doors and found himself in a carpeted area with a reception desk in the center and office doors all along the walls of the large room.

No one was at the reception desk, but he set off a little bell as he stepped through the doors, and almost instantly a short man with narrow, deep-set eyes stuck his head out of an open door. It was Joe. He was smiling and waved for Derek to join him. When Derek stepped inside Joe's office, he was shocked to find the back wall consisting of a big window overlooking the pond and fountain that he drove by as he entered the building's parking lot everyday. Joe noticed Derek's wide-eye look and smiled broadly. "Nice, huh?" he asked.

"Very nice," Derek responded. He shook Joe's hand and looked around the office. It was nicely appointed with pictures everywhere — on the room's ample shelves, on the desk and on the credenza. They were family scenes featuring Joe, a woman who must be his wife, and children of all ages. It was clear that Joe was quite the family man, and Derek couldn't help notice that Joe's wife was an attractive woman. "You've got quite a family, Joe," Derek said.

"And I love showing them off," Joe said with a big smile and a sweeping gesture that took in the whole room. "Of course, I don't get many visitors other than my staff," he added. "Here, make yourself comfortable at the table and I'll get you a soda. What's your pleasure?"

"A cola is fine," said Derek as he pulled out one of six chairs at a large table in the right corner of the room. Joe was gone and back in a flash, carrying two sodas. He set them down in front of Derek, stepped over to his desk, opened a drawer, took out a lunch bag and then took the seat on Derek's right. "Glad you could join me today," Joe said. "I'm covering the lunch hour for my department today, but to tell you the truth I do it pretty often. I like the peace and quiet time to catch up on my reading."

"Oops," said Derek with a grin, not sure if Joe was offering a subtle dig about Derek interrupting his plans.

"Oh no, like I said, I'm *glad* you're here," Joe explained. "I just meant to say that having company for lunch makes it a special occasion. And the opportunity to talk about what I get out of being an active Christian makes it doubly special. So I feel blessed that you could get down here today."

Derek felt at ease in Joe's company, and he was impressed by what he had gathered about Joe's circumstances. He had a nice office, nice family and certainly had plenty of social skills. "Well, I'm glad we could get together too," Derek responded. "But before we talk about anything else, tell me a bit about this family that has overtaken your office.

"My family is very important to me," said Joe. "It's not the center of my life — God is. But it's right next to God. And, in fact, my family is my main path *to* God and my biggest grace *from* Him. Both God and my family are more important to me than life itself, although life is an awesome gift too," Joe explained.

"I see a lot of water and trees in most of these photos. Do you get together somewhere up in the north woods?" Derek asked, taken by the beauty of the setting in most of the photos.

"Yes, that's our place up north," Joe explained. "We bought it several years ago. It was just woods then. We started going up whenever we could get away, almost every weekend in the summer. We stayed in a tent and did a little work on every visit. It gave us a lot of opportunities to be together and to work together as a family — and it was a lot cheaper than taking the crew to an amusement park. Meanwhile, back here in town, we watched for people who were remodeling their homes and throwing out old windows, siding, doors, shutters, anything. When we found something that looked like we could use, we hauled it up to our land in a trailer and tried to integrate it into our project. To make a long story short, we started 15 years ago and today we have a cottage and a bunkhouse up there. The kids and their friends are up there all the time with us."

"I don't mean to pry, but how many kids do you have?" Derek asked. "There seems to be an awful lot of them, judging from these photos.

Joe laughed. "Don't let the photos fool you. We're not running an orphanage, although my wife used to talk about trying to do something like that. You see so many kids in the photos because of the children's friends. We had just four children ourselves, but each of them shows up about 30 times in these photos.

"Well, they are obviously bringing you great joy," Derek said.

"Oh yes, they are the joy of my life. But there's been pain too," Joe said, letting his gaze drop to the floor. "I said we *had* four children. Now we have just three. We lost a child about 10 years ago to a dreadful illness. It really tore us apart. Words can't describe the horror of that first family Christmas without her. We cried and cried and cried. It was so sad. And I think because we all reminded each other of our loss, we drifted apart. We found excuses to be out of the house and to be busy on weekends so we couldn't go to the lake. After being so close, it was such an awful change. I was so bitter, so angry, that I just made my wife's pain worse. But gratefully, we gradually came to see what was happening and began to slowly pull back together again. The pain never entirely goes away. It's like a little hole in me, right down here," Joe said, gesturing toward his stomach. "But we are at a point where we can enjoy and celebrate life together again, and I'm so grateful for that."

Derek was a little uncomfortable pursuing a topic that was so obviously painful to Joe, but he couldn't help himself. He could imagine nothing worse than to lose one of his children, and he wanted to understand how someone could cope with such a loss. He had been to a few funerals of youngsters in his lifetime when he couldn't find a way to avoid them. But he had never had the opportunity to listen to how parents cope with such an inconsolable loss. "I don't want to add to your pain, Joe, but can you tell me more about the anger you mentioned?"

Joe looked past Derek out the window, obviously trying to keep the tears in his eyes from welling over onto his cheeks. "It's no problem, Derek. I don't mind talking about it. I was angry at everyone, I suppose, but mostly at God. I said to Him, 'Why is this happening to me? I've always tried to be good. Why are you betraying me? Why are you so cruel?'"

"And did you get an answer?" Derek asked, both wondering and skeptical at the same time.

"Eventually I did," said Joe. "I won't go into all the details here because it's such a personal thing that it's hard to put into words. But while I cursed God and added to my family's pain, I slowly began to notice that all the forces helping me to deal with my loss were coming from my church. That opened a little window for me that eventually became a big door I could walk through — back to a sense of meaning and purpose in life. I was mad at God, so mad.

But I started to see that He loved me nevertheless, and He was sending everyone who was trying to help me cope. Eventually — and I confess it was not easy — I decided to accept His love and step fully back into the fold.

"Since then I've been able to enjoy the many blessings I do have in this life and I've been able to more fully realize that this life is not the end of the story. It's just the beginning. So I enjoy each day as God gives me to have this day, and I look forward to a life beyond this life where all of us will be united — my parents and grandparents as well as my dear daughter. I want to be ready when that day comes, so I don't want to squander what God gives me to work with while I'm here. That's the big picture for me. But hey, I've been talking for a long time, Derek, and our purpose today is to answer your questions. So why don't you jump in here?"

Derek chuckled. "You *are* answering my questions — some of them anyway — and I guess you're doing it before I even knew I was going to ask them. Listen, Joe, what you're saying is helping me a lot."

"But you do have questions, right?" Joe asked.

"Well, I do and I don't," said Derek. "I'm not trying to be coy. I'm just trying to put it all together. As I told Tom, life started out pretty good for me. You could say I spent a lot of time in the fast lane. But now I seem to be just drifting. Nothing really excites me. I'm not selling like I used to. My kids are happy to ignore me. My wife has her own interests that seem to keep her busy — and some of it is stuff I couldn't care a hoot about. I've got some buddies, but if I dropped over dead today I'm not sure they would lose much more than a night out together going to my wake with their wives. So what's it all about? What am I doing here? What's the point? Where's the big payoff, the big win? Those are my questions, Joe. Who's got answers to questions like that?"

"So you're not getting *any* answers?" Joe asked.

"Well, I am and I'm not," said Derek. "I mean, I don't want to be coy with this either. In fact, Tom has been a big help. And so were Jerry and Mary. At least they seem to have the answers for themselves. And I'm pretty sure their answers have relevance for me. I just haven't put it all together for myself yet."

"Sounds to me like you're a *Christian under construction* — just like the rest of us," Joe said.

"Maybe so," Derek responded, pleased to think that he might have something in common with Tom and his friends that others could see. "But if that's the case, I've got a long way to go. In fact, I don't think I even have a roof over me yet. And I'm afraid it could starting raining or snowing any minute."

Joe let out a laugh. He liked the analogy. "No roof, huh? Well we can't leave it that way, can we?" he declared in mock seriousness. "I guess we better get to work this very minute."

Derek laughed too, mostly at the thought that with a little effort and guidance he could get rid of that gnawing, unsettled feeling that had come to haunt him. On his own he hadn't accomplished a thing — except to increase his level of frustration. "Joe," he asked, "are you saying that if we add a board here and a board there, so to speak, pretty soon I'll be good as new? Is that what you're proposing?"

"Wouldn't that be nice?" said Joe. "If it worked that way I could have spared myself several years in the dumps. I don't think we can set a timeline. But we can get started with a board here and a board there, as you put it, and hope for the best."

Derek liked Joe's can-do attitude. It was the kind of feeling that had kept him going so many times before when he was alone on the road. He would tell himself that he was just "between sales" as he fought to avoid panic over the fear that he might have made his last sale in life. But lately Derek had experienced fewer and fewer "can-do" moments and he wished he could have more. Now he felt that Joe's attitude was contagious. "Okay," he said. "Let's get started and hope for the best."

"Where do you want to begin?" asked Joe.

Derek was ready for the question. "Joe, I'm beginning to see that I am going to have to connect many of the dots myself because they are my own dots. But I can also see that you and the others have a lot to offer me. You're all good models of people who have their lives together and who care about other people. But mostly what I get from you is a sense of hope for myself. If your lives make sense to you, mine can make sense to me. So why don't you just tell me your story and I'll jump in when I've got something to say?"

Joe was looking him in the eyes and smiling broadly. "I'm good with that, Derek," he said. "Let's get going then, and don't be shy about jumping in whenever it suits you. There's just one thing I want to clarify: You won't have to connect the dots yourself. It may seem like you have to now. But the day will come when you look back and see that you've had a lot of help with it. I promise. And more important, *He* promised. But that will all become clear in good time. Let me go back a bit and start a little closer to the beginning."

Derek nodded, took a bite out of his sandwich, settled back in his chair and lifted the cola to his lips. He was ready and eager to do some serious, active listening.

"You know there was never much flash to me," Joe started. "Back in school I used to envy guys like you who always seemed to be in the spotlight and were even chased by the prettiest girls. I knew I was no prize. I didn't get a single A in high school. I went out for a few sports but never got to play. I don't even think any girls noticed me except when they wanted someone to mock or to pity. I remember once, in my freshman year, I was bursting with confidence. I had grown four inches over the summer and had gotten contacts. My nerd days were behind me, I was sure. So I decided to ask Marcie, that cute cheerleader, if she would go to homecoming with me. She laughed, touched my shoulder and said, "Oh Joe, you are so cute" — like you would say it to a puppy. Then she walked away laughing and shaking her head. It was the last time I ever talked to a cheerleader. I used to think if I ever saw my name up in lights, the sign would say, "Joe Schmo, average in every way.""

Derek was uncomfortable at the thought of how he had treated others who weren't in his clique in high school. It wasn't that he was mean. Generally, he just wasn't aware that they even existed — except when they complimented him after a big game or envied the good looking "accessories" he had hanging on his arm. He was pretty sure back then that most of the kids not in his clique wanted more than anything to be him. Listening to Joe, he decided not to interject and just keep listening.

"Anyway, I had an undistinguished student career and I looked ahead to what you might call 'bleak prospects.' I didn't get into an elite school. I didn't get into any college. Heck, I never even thought of applying. I saw a job here advertised in the paper the week after our high school graduation and I took it. It was a grace from God. The people in maintenance here turned out to be a lot nicer than my peers in school.

"Oh, they teased me and played a few 'new guy' tricks on me. But they were always careful to let me know that they took me seriously and cared about my feelings. It was a big change for me. Gradually I settled in and began to feel a sense of accomplishment. I guess I was still a nerd, but I wasn't *just* a nerd. I was a guy who could contribute. And so I did. Eventually, I realized that it was important for me to do a good job — no matter what the job. Why? Because when I did a really good job, I earned both self-respect and the respect of those who mattered to me. In a sense, I found a family here.

"Over the first few months, I found a couple of mentors. I watched them — guys like me, but older, with their feet on the ground. I could see that they were happy. They really had wonderful lives. Their wives and children brought them great joy and satisfaction. There were others, of course. Big shots. They went for the attention. But working side by side, I could see that they weren't as happy as the other guys.

"When you're waxing a long hallway or cleaning toilets, you get a lot of time to think, and I thought about what it would take to make me happy. I decided it isn't winning the lottery or getting a big windfall inheritance. It isn't about getting more and more all the time — more money, more attention, more women, whatever. It is a matter of learning how to appreciate what you have. It is a matter of being grateful for everything good that is given to you in life. It is a matter of showing your gratitude by living each day as best you can.

"I was never a flashy guy, so maybe all of this came a little easier to me. You know the story of the tortoise and the hare — the slow turtle and the quick rabbit? I guess I got over the fact that I wasn't a rabbit and I would never be a rabbit. I was a turtle. But I also came to realize that if I did the things a turtle did, over and over, day in and day out, I could experience victory. My mentors here encouraged me to take every kind of technical class and study program that was offered. I was reluctant at first because I had never done well in the classroom. But they really pushed me, and eventually I gave in. When I did, good things happened. I felt comfortable with the topics and I did well. That gave me more confidence and eventually I was certified to handle every system in the building.

"I came here not thinking much of myself, thinking I was really second-rate or worse. But I was blessed to meet the kinds of people who really cared for me, who really nurtured me. With their support and guidance I came to see that I was just a slow bloomer. I also came to see that having a good life came down to making a good life. I realized I didn't have to do anything spectacular — which was a big relief to me, because I don't think I'm engineered for spectacular performances. I just had to do my best at what really mattered to me, day in and day out, and my life would be full and satisfying. I guess I decided that the best rule for me is *don't break any rules*. I can't say I have always lived up to that, but it does sort of sum up my life.

Derek decided this was a good place to jump in. "That sounds easy enough. Why didn't I think of it?"

"Well Derek, I'm here to tell you it isn't as easy as it sounds. And you probably didn't think of it because it sounds pretty boring. But let me assure you. It doesn't have to be boring. Keeping the rules — at least the important rules, the big ones that come from God — can be very exciting and fulfilling. But I'll admit, it takes some time. And more than that, it takes some help."

"So who helps you stay on the straight and narrow?" Derek asked.

"I have two answers to that," Joe replied, "and I think both are essential. The first is my wife, Joan. We met at the mall about a year or so after I got out of high school and started working here. I was looking for something to buy my mother for Mother's Day. To tell you the truth, it was also a peace offering, because she was getting fed up with me living at home and not contributing anything but dirty laundry and dishes. So I was looking for something special — something very out of character for me — and Joan mistook me for a considerate son. What a break! If it wasn't exactly love at first sight for me, it was certainly a strong attraction. She was cute and funny and so considerate.

"I caught another break too. I mistook her training to be a helpful sales clerk with her having a real personal interest in me. Imagine — *me!* She was so nice to me that I was ready to buy out the whole store. Fortunately, she just did her job and helped me pick out something that made sense for my budget and absolutely thrilled my mother. I've been listening to her advice ever since, and it has served me well.

"Oh, and I caught one more break that night — literally. As she was checking me out, her supervisor told her to take her break. So I asked, barely able to get out the words, "Can I buy you a soda?" When she looked surprised, I was embarrassed and stammered something about "just to say thanks for helping me pick out a gift." She took that as another sign that I was an especially thoughtful guy and took me up on my offer. Fortunately, she's been misreading me that way ever since and I usually don't have the gumption to disappoint her.

"As we talked that night I got the courage to ask her out. It turned out that the night I suggested was a night that she had a conflict with something at her church. Then, just as I was about to conclude that my usual bad luck had returned, she said she could bring a guest, and she asked if I wanted to go with her. I hadn't been to a church in a few years and it wasn't on my list of places to get to soon. But I would have gone to war for her, so church didn't seem like such a big deal. Know what? We still belong to that church today.

"And that gets me to the second thing that keeps me on the straight and narrow or gets me back when I stumble off the path — my membership in Christian communities. There's my church and the Bible study group here at work. Over the years we've built some lasting friendships through our church. We've got other friends too. We don't limit our socializing to people from our church. In fact, we've made some good friends up at the lake. Over the year we'll see a lot of different people. And I bet I don't have to tell you, it's a lot easier making friends individually than as a couple."

"You've got that right," Derek interjected. "It's to the point that I dread hearing my wife Sally say she's met someone and would like us to go out with her and her husband. I can almost guarantee that I won't get along with the husband. And vice-versa. If I meet a guy I like and we go out with him and his wife, it's almost a lead pipe cinch that Sally won't like the wife. But what's that got to do with church?"

"We have found the opportunities our church gives us to meet and socialize with other couples in large groups has helped us slowly build some good relationships with other couples over the years. And I can't tell you how helpful it is to be part of a network of people whose lives and values are similar to your own. For example, it's good to know that you're not the only parents who lay down rules for your children. It can help a lot when a group of parents with similar values put their heads together to develop some common rules — and then stick together when the kids stretch them and try to break them.

"When Joan and I have had difficulties — and every couple has them — it helped me to be around men who were devoted to being good husbands and fathers. We all weaken, but in the right company we don't have to fall. The others hold us up, usually without even being aware of it. The value of a good support system often doesn't even occur to us until we see a friend's life fall apart for lack of one. Then we can see how God has blessed us with the right sort of network of relationships. But, of course, we're free to go another way, to make other choices. And many do."

Derek had to jump in. "Joe, I hope this doesn't offend you, and if it does I hope you'll forgive me. But I have to confess that hanging around church-types just doesn't sound like much fun to me. Even if I belonged to a church and participated regularly in its worship services, I can't see myself doing a lot of things with other members — maybe couples, but not just the guys, if you know what I mean."

"I think I do, Derek," Joe smiled. "Remember, I felt that way once about church myself. But I also have to say that gradually, over the years, I have met some great guys. Some of us like to fish. There's a bowling team from the church, but that doesn't interest me. I like going to the races, and one guy from my church joins me and some guys from work here. Joan and I belong to a card club of church members. But we skip the bus trips some of the folks like to take. The point I'm trying to make is that the church didn't force any socializing on us. It just expanded our choices. We went to the things we thought we would enjoy and spent time with people we thought would be enjoyable. We never felt obligated. But I see now how it has made a huge and wonderful difference in our lives — and helped hold us up at those times when we were headed down."

Derek chuckled. "You said it 'expanded your choices.' I have to confess that I never thought of church membership as expanding anything. I guess I'm still struggling with the memories of hearing *don't do this, don't do that* all the time about everything. So when I hear the word 'church,' I think of shrinking choices — or no choices at all."

It was Joe's turn to chuckle. "I know what you're talking about, Derek," he said. "Been there, thought that. But home was a lot like that for us when we were little too, just one rule after another, and most of us didn't reject our parents. Instead, if God gives us the time, we try to build good adult relationships with them. And sometimes God gives us so much time we end up being a parent to our parents. My point is, don't confuse your childhood experiences with adult opportunities. And when you look at church as an adult opportunity, I think you'll be surprised — pleasantly surprised. Anyway, you asked about the big positive forces in my life, and now you know about the two biggest ones. Maybe it's different for other people, but I can only speak from my experience."

"And I'm grateful you did," Derek said. "Don't confuse my skepticism with disbelief. You've given me a lot to think about, and I'm grateful. I really am."

"Let me give you one more thing then, if you've got the time," Joe offered. Derek was beginning to feel pressed to get back to contacting clients, but he looked at the clock and realized he still had a few minutes to spare. "Sure, go ahead," he replied.

Joe continued. "Remember my motto from high school? *Average in every way*. Well, church has given me an opportunity to be more than that, Derek. It has connected me to some remarkable ministries and given me a chance to see that I do have some important contributions to make in this world. I'll give you just one example. Several years ago Joan and I had started talking about taking a vacation in the Caribbean. It was going to be expensive so we had been saving our money for almost a year when we heard about a church program that took people down to a Caribbean island for 10 days to help with building projects. The accommodations weren't plush, but the price was reasonable and it looked like an opportunity to do a little good, so we decided to go. It was a remarkable adventure. We met wonderful people, really got a taste of a very different culture, and when we left there was a bright new roof on the old two-room building that was their school. I can't tell you the sense of accomplishment we got from that. The only things brighter than that roof were the smiles on the people's faces as they waved goodbye to us at the end of our stay.

"In my wildest dreams I had no idea that ol' Joe here, average in every way, was blessed with gifts that made life better for a whole village of people. And Joan had some great stories to tell about her experiences tutoring the children. Everyone there was just so grateful to us. And we found ourselves so grateful for the opportunity to share our gifts and to feel so loved and appreciated. It was, as management around here likes to say, a real win-win deal.

"Anyway, we've been back several times. The old two-room school now has four more rooms, all under a good roof, and I helped put in a new well and restrooms on my last visit. Meanwhile, some of Joan's first students are tutors themselves now, and two have even gone on to study to become teachers. Can you imagine? I don't want to sound too proud, Derek. And I hope you will forgive me this conceit. But I'm awestruck that God has given someone as ordinary as me the chance to contribute and leave such a legacy for a whole village of people half a world away. Without the opportunities presented to me at church, my life would have been lived on an entirely different level.

Joe's story caught Derek completely by surprise. "I'm amazed. I had no idea that church could open doors like that," he admitted. "I guess I just didn't associate the notion of church with expanding life's opportunities. You have really put me on to something, Joe, and I'm grateful."

"Well, if there's anything else I can do for you, let me know. A lot of weekends I'm gone to the lake. But I haven't figured out yet how to afford spending all my weekdays there too, so until I do you can generally find me right here."

"Thanks, I appreciate that. I really do," said Derek. "And we'll see each other again, I'm sure of it. But I better run. I've got some calls to make or they won't let me back in here."

They both chuckled. There had been some layoffs, and neither one of them had to be reminded that the pressure was on to perform, especially in the sales department where it was easy to measure productivity. "Keep your head down and your orders up," Joe said with a smile.

"Got it. Thanks again," Derek said as he stepped out the door and down the hall toward the elevator. Suddenly he realized that they hadn't even talked about the Bible study and prayer group. He smiled. That gave him an excuse to get back to Tom and continue their dialogue. He decided to check in with him first thing the next morning.

GETTING STARTED

In the morning Derek arrived at the office a little early and headed for the elevator. He knew that Tom would be in his office, and he wasn't surprised when Tom welcomed him with a big smile and gestured for him to take a seat. "Did you get a chance to visit with Joe?" Tom asked as he stepped around his desk and took the chair next to Derek's.

"I sure did, and I wanted to thank you for putting me on to him," Derek replied. "He's turned out to be quite a guy. I found what he had to say very helpful."

"So what can I do for you today?" asked Tom.

"Well, it's funny you should ask. But I realized right after I left Joe's office that we had gotten so involved in talking about his life and the work he and his wife do overseas that I forgot to ask him about the Bible study and prayer group here at the office," Derek said. "I've been getting a little more interested in that as I've been making the rounds of your friends."

"Good, let's talk about that for a moment. It's really pretty simple. We meet once a week on Wednesdays in a little room in the back of the little café next door. There could be as many as a dozen of us, but given everyone's schedule, usually about six to 10 are on hand. We take turns being leaders, and the leader selects a passage from the Bible to read. First we order our food and then read the passage. Then we discuss it for about 10 or 15 minutes until our food arrives. After we eat we pray. That's pretty simple too. We share our intentions and ask everyone to pray for them. Then we pray for our intentions that we keep deep in our hearts — you know, things we're not comfortable sharing at the moment. Then we thank God for his many blessings, ask him to watch over us and our loved ones in the days to come, and then we head back to the office. We're back here in an hour. Are you asking about it because you might want to join us, Derek?"

"Well, that's part of it," Derek replied. "I don't think I'm ready just yet. But I admit I'm interested, and so I just wanted to know what I'd be getting myself into. Would it be okay to join you later instead of right now?"

"Derek, you're welcome any time," Tom replied. "There's no sign-up. No dues. And we don't pass the hat either. You just show up and all it costs you is the price of the lunch you order. If you become a regular, you'll be asked to lead the group eventually. But if you're not comfortable with that, just decline the offer. It's no big deal. Some of our regulars never want to lead."

"On that basis, it's hard to say no," Derek smiled. "But I still want to wait a bit. I've got a plan and I wanted to see what you think of it."

"Fire away," said Tom.

"I'm taking Sally out to dinner for our wedding anniversary tomorrow night. These dinners have gotten pretty superficial over the years. We look for a new spot, something nice. We order. Then I give her a nice piece of jewelry. She opens it, oohs ands ahs for a few moments, thanks me, says she loves me and reaches across the table to take my hand and squeeze it. Then we're back to talking about kids and bills and whatever, trying not to argue because it's our anniversary. To tell you the truth, I think we're both relieved when it's over. We do it every year, so we're doing it again. She even went ahead and made reservations at some new place she's heard others rave about.

"But I've been thinking," Derek went on. "I want this year to be different. I don't want the restaurant, the food and the jewelry to be the center of our conversation. I want to share with her the things you and I have been talking about. And I want to tell her what I've been hearing from your friends around here. I want to draw her out, get her to talk about what she really feels about us, where she would like to see our relationship and family life heading. I want to listen and take what she says into account. But then I'd like to offer to start going to church with her and taking all the kids with us. I don't want to promise too much because I don't know how I'll do with this. And I hate to think what my golfing buddies are going to say about me dropping out of their foursome. But I've been thinking, I should put first things first. And if I want a good life with Sally and the kids, I should start trying to build that life now."

Derek sat back in his chair. There was a little smile, almost a smirk, on his face. "What do you think about that, buddy?" he asked.

Tom paused a moment before replying, just to let a little suspense build and add to the occasion. Then he spoke: "Sounds like a plan to me." He paused for another moment before continuing. "Can I ask a question?"

"Sure, go for it," Derek said, obviously pleased with his plan and the reception it had gotten.

"Can you tell me what moved you to decide on this plan?" he asked.

"Not really," Derek chuckled. "I mean, I guess it's just everything all of you have told me. And more than that, it's what you're *doing*. You all seem so darn happy. I don't mean that in a superficial sense. I mean you all seem to be happy *deep down*. I've been thinking about all of you. Your backgrounds are all different and your circumstances are all different. And some of you have had some real heartbreaks. Yet, all of you are coping. In fact, you really seem content. I don't mean in a self-satisfied way. Clearly, all of you believe you have more work to do — on yourselves and on the world. But you also have the sense that you are doing it. That your life has direction, a purpose. I think I've been missing that."

Tom was smiling more broadly now. "I'm glad we could be of help. I really like your idea about how to make your anniversary special tomorrow night, and I'll be praying for you. In fact, we could pray right now, if you're not uncomfortable with that."

Derek looked a little perplexed. "No, that's okay. I mean, I guess I have to start somewhere. So what do I do?"

"Not much," Tom said. "Just bow your head and close your eyes and make my words your own, as much as they reflect what you're feeling right now." Then Tom bowed his own head, closed his eyes and began.

"Dear Heavenly Father, we, your humble servants, ask your blessings on us and all that we care about. We are weak but you are strong. Please forgive us our faults and shortcomings. Please share your strength and be our guide as we try to do the right thing, as we struggle to be all that you created us to be, as we strive to live faithful to your calling for us and to care, as you would care, for those whom you have entrusted to us. And Lord, we especially ask

that you and your only son bless the union of Derek and Sally. Help them grow closer tomorrow and every day as they labor to reflect your love in their love for one another. Amen."

"Amen," Derek added, a little surprised at himself. "I guess it's all coming back to me," he joked as he looked up at Tom.

"You're covered, Derek. I think you're a natural," Tom teased. "When you get a chance, let me know how it goes tomorrow night. And remember, I'll be praying for you. In fact, we all will, if you let me share your plans with the rest of the group here."

"Hold up on that for now, Tom," Derek replied. "Wait, you said the group prays for everybody's silent intentions too, didn't you?"

"Yes, I did," Tom replied. "And that will be mine at lunch today, Derek. Sure you don't want to join us?"

"Not yet. Give me a little time with this, Tom," Derek said. "I know better than to go it alone. But I want to start with Sally and see how it goes with her. I just have this sense that this is something that should begin with us."

"I like your thinking," Tom said. "Stay in touch." They shook hands and Derek headed for the elevator.

BREAKING THROUGH

Derek's sales responsibilities kept him on the road all week long for the next several weeks. After a week Tom started to wonder why he hadn't seen his friend. He began to worry that maybe Derek's anniversary proposal hadn't gone as well as both of them had wished. But then the receptionist inadvertently put his mind at ease. "Your buddy must really be busy," she said one morning when Tom walked by. "My buddy?" Tom asked, confused by the reference. "That Derek, the cute guy who stops by to visit occasionally," she explained. "He must really be busy. He faxed in his last expense report and asked us to make a direct deposit to his account. Said he would be back in town only for weekends for another month or two," the receptionist explained.

"That's busy, all right," Tom agreed as he headed back toward his office. Tom was relieved to know there was a good reason why he hadn't seen Derek since the two had discussed Derek's anniversary plans. At the same time, he wondered how Derek's extensive travels would affect his efforts to build deeper bonds at home. It was another two months before he found out.

Suddenly one morning before anyone else was in his department Tom looked up from his work and there was Derek. "Hey buddy, got a minute?" Derek asked. His tone was casual. "Sure," Tom replied in the same casual way, stepping around his desk and motioning Derek to take the chair he always used. "Can I get you a cup of coffee?"

"No," Derek said. "I only have a minute. They're killing us in sales. But at least it's finally getting busy again. We're back to worrying how we can fill orders rather than how we will ever find them, and I have to tell you, I'd rather have this set of problems. But it's rush, rush, rush."

"I wondered why you hadn't stopped by. I even left a voice mail message a week or so after you were up the last time," Tom said. "But then the receptionist said you faxed in your expenses with a note that said you'd be on the road for at least a couple of months, so I stopped worrying about you."

"Well, I'm glad you didn't worry. But I hope you still prayed," Derek said.

"I did that," Tom replied, glad to hear that still mattered to Derek.

"I knew I could count on you," Derek said. "But most of all, I'm more convinced than ever I can count on God."

"So things have been going well for you?" Tom asked, interested but not wanting to appear nosy.

"Yes, Tom, they have — beyond expectations, really. Sally and I had a great anniversary dinner. I admit I felt awkward when I first started to talk to her about my feelings. And I had no idea how I was going to get to the part about being interested in going to church with her and the whole family. But once I started, she was so different that everything just flowed, almost naturally it seemed. She liked the jewelry and thanked me for it. But we didn't discuss it or the other things her friends had gotten for their anniversaries, like we have in years past. We focused on us — on our hopes, our dreams, and yes, on our disappointments. After a while, we talked about the kids too. But it was different than before. In the past, it seemed like we would just jump from thing to thing, and we usually ended up focusing on the aggravations. You know, all the things they say and do — and don't do — that drive us nuts. I never found that very gratifying.

"But that night, on our anniversary, we talked about them differently. I really can't explain it. But it was gratifying, even when we touched on the inevitable aggravations. Tom, it felt like we were a team — no, more than a team, really. It felt like we were *one* again. And we saw that our children were our greatest treasure. Funny, words can't explain it. But I get the sense that you know what I'm talking about. Anyway, I had no idea so much was going on inside of Sally's head. She really had some concerns about our son. In the past I probably would have changed the subject or argued with her. But this time I listened and I found myself really appreciating hearing her talk about those concerns and the other things on her mind.

"And Tom, you know what else? She really does care for me, in spite of how I can be such a jerk sometimes. I would have been angry to hear it before, but at one point she said she prays for me every day. I was so gratified — and I told her so. Of course, that surprised her. She said she never mentioned it before because she thought it would make me angry. Can you imagine? No, don't answer that. The point is, *I* can imagine it. And I'm not proud of it. But she still loves me. So what can I say? Life is good."

Tom was curious. "What about all the travel? That can't be the best thing for you."

"Funny you should ask, Tom. I would have thought that too. Sally has never liked me traveling. It certainly doesn't help me get involved in what the kids are doing. And as you know, it's also been a source of temptation for me from time to time. So you would think that all this travel would have been a real wrench in the gears for us. But you know what? It hasn't been that way at all. I mean, it hasn't been easy. But we're handling it differently now, and I think it could even be a plus for us.

"It used to be that when I'd get home Friday night from a week on the road, I'd throw my bags on the bed, mix a drink, drop myself down on the couch and start to veg out. I mean, that's what I'd been pointing to all the way home. The kids would get the message. And if they didn't get it on their own, I'd make sure they got it. I'd say, 'Hey, give me a break. I'm tired. Go find something to do.' And you know what they did?"

"They found something to do that didn't include you," Tom replied.

"That's right. They found a lot of things to do that didn't include me. And pretty soon they didn't even have to be reminded to do those other things. They ignored me just like I made it clear I wanted to ignore them. I mean, it wasn't that I didn't love them. I did. But I had these expectations that I would get home and enjoy peace and quiet and maybe a game on TV. My plan didn't consider them or their needs. So soon enough their plans weren't considering me. But that's different now — or at least it's getting to be different."

"How so?" asked Tom, if for no reason than to let Derek know he was interested in hearing more of his story.

"Now I focus on what's most important — and that's Sally and the kids. So on my way home I see myself greeting them, hugging them, and then doing something with them, something that will give me a chance to catch up on what they've been doing while I've been gone. I know they love pizza. So one week I'll focus on taking them to a favorite pizza place. Another time I knew they wanted to see a movie. It looked like something we all might enjoy, so I asked Sally on the phone to stall the kids until Friday night and we could all go together. It was great, and I caught up on their activities over ice cream sundaes after the movie.

"And Tom, that's another thing. While I'm on the road, I stay in touch more often. I try to call every night. The only times I miss are if I'm in an earlier time zone and I have to go with a client to a late game or something like that. I started packing a book or two about something that really interests me. I've always liked popular fiction. But would you believe I've started packing books about parenting, personal development and even spiritual development too? Now that I've started looking for it, I'm amazed that there is so much out there. If I take a fiction title, usually it will be a book Sally has read and recommends, so when I call home we can talk about that too.

"A couple of weeks ago I came across a book about being a better spouse, and do you know what I did? I bought two identical copies! Sally thought I was nuts. But we both read a chapter every night before I called, and then we shared our thoughts about what we read. I found myself really looking forward to that time together. Tom, I really have the sense that we are becoming good friends — again, after all these years.

"Yeah, but what are you going to do with two copies of the same book?" Tom teased.

"We'll do what we do with a lot of the books we're getting. We'll donate them to our church reading room. The volunteers there tell me they're popular with other church members. Somebody even came in the other day, returned a book, and then asked, 'Has that Derek guy donated any new titles lately? He's got pretty good taste.' It cracked me up."

"So you're going to church these days?" Tom asked.

"Yes, that's a regular part of our new Sunday routine — *especially* if I have to be on the road all week," Derek said, anticipating Tom's next question. "Sally and I talked about it and we decided the children could have Saturdays to do what they want, so long as it's healthy, and we would be supportive. If it's something just for kids, we make ourselves available to chauffeur. If it's a family activity, we work it into our schedules. Then on Sundays we all eat breakfast and go to church to worship together. The kids weren't crazy about it at first, but it's part of our routine now and I think we all appreciate it in our own way. In fact, a couple of weeks ago I had to stay out on the road, couldn't get home for the weekend. But Sally and the kids stuck to the routine, and she told me later on the way home from church one of the kids said, 'I didn't like church today.' So Sally asked why, and she was told, 'Because Daddy wasn't with us.' When she told me that, I almost cried, Tom. It wasn't that many months ago when I wondered if they even cared I was alive. Now I hear that they actually miss me! Tell you what, I couldn't wait to get home and give 'em all a big hug."

"I think you're telling me 'so far, so good' then?" Tom asked.

"I think I'm telling you 'so far, so great!'" Derek replied. "I'm really feeling on track again. And I can't tell you how grateful I am that I didn't procrastinate when I started to get cold feet at dinner on our anniversary. If we hadn't gotten started on this then, I don't know what all this traveling would have done to my marriage and family life. In fact, I dread to think about that. It couldn't have been good, Tom. So I guess the good Lord looks out for us."

"He does when we let him," Tom chimed in.

"Yes, we have to cooperate. I can see that," says Derek. "But I sure can't take credit for how well things have gone in these last few months. I mean, I just do my best, try to stay on track, and pray regularly for God's help and guidance. Then I try to stay out of the way and let God be God. And Tom, it's amazing."

"So you're glad you started joining Sally on Sunday mornings?" Tom asked with a tone of obvious understatement that made Derek laugh.

"I am! Though I have to tell you, the other morning when it was snowing and the wind was howling, the *Church of the Inner Spring* looked pretty good to me. But once I got up and had breakfast with the family, I was so grateful for them that I actually wanted to go to church and thank God for all my blessings. The feeling surprised me. Of course, it's not all sea shells and bon-bons."

"It's not what?" said Tom, not familiar with the expression Derek used.

Derek laughed. "Sea shells and bon-bons. Al McGuire, who was a colorful basketball coach at Marquette University and later a TV commentator, used that expression to mean something like 'perfectly wonderful.' I have to tell you, going to church isn't always perfectly wonderful for me.

"It's not?" Tom asked. "What's the problem?"

"Well frankly, sometimes I find it boring. My mind drifts. And then I find myself asking why I bothered to go. A few weeks ago I bought a business book called *Raving Fans: A Revolutionary Approach to Customer Service* by Ken Blanchard and Sheldon Bowles. I was talking to Sally about it and later when the topic turned to church, I told her, 'Honey, I guess I've got a way to go before I'm a *raving fan* of church services.' She laughed and agreed. But then she told me how much she appreciates having me there, praying beside her, with all of us together, and I had to admit that makes it all worthwhile even when the sermon gets a little dry."

"Sounds like it's not a big problem," Tom offered.

"Actually, it's not really a problem at all. And the benefits far outweigh my occasional moments of boredom. Now that she knows I'm supportive of her, Sally has been attending the meetings of a women's group at the church once a week. She says she really appreciates the adult companionship especially when I'm gone. And the children are both involved in the church's youth ministry program. Sometimes that means a lot more driving for Sally or me on Saturday or Sunday afternoons. But sometimes it means more time alone for just the two of us too. So that's a blessing on at least two levels, if you know what I mean."

"I think I do, Derek. And I'm glad to hear things are going so well for you, despite all the travel," Tom said.

"There's one more thing if you've got just another moment," Derek interjected.

"Go for it," Tom said. It was getting late and he had a report due by mid-morning. But he didn't want it to look like he was rushing Derek.

"Are you still accepting visitors at your Wednesday noon meetings next door?" Derek asked.

"Yes, we are. The welcome mat is always out," Tom replied. "Are you interested in stopping by?"

"I've thought about it a lot, and I guess I would like to give it a try," Derek said. "I know this transition that I'm trying to make is not something that I can accomplish by myself. I need Sally's encouragement and support. It doesn't hurt that the kids are on board with the process too. And I realize that I never would have even started down this path without the support and encouragement of you and the people you had me talk with. I think I'm headed in the right direction, but it's clear to me that I need to build up a support system for myself if I want to continue growing.

"I'll still be traveling a lot so I won't become a regular, at least for the time being. But I can start showing up when I'm in town. If nothing else I'd like to see all the people you sent me to and thank them. And it might surprise them to finally see me there after all this time."

"It might surprise them," Tom agreed. "But I'm absolutely certain it will do something else."

"What's that?" asked Derek, perplexed.

"It will please them, Derek. It will please them to no end."

Derek smiled. "It's a date, then, buddy. See you all Wednesday noon."

And he did see them. Over and over again. Whenever he was in town on Wednesdays.

Then one day while Derek was preparing his monthly expense report to take upstairs, he got a call from Tom. "I've got a guy in my office that I'd like you to talk to about why you're a regular at our Wednesday luncheons, Derek. Can you see him?" Tom asked.

"Send him right down," Derek said. "I'm glad you called, and I'll be happy to try and serve him."

ACKNOWLEDGMENTS

The debts I have incurred in getting this little book into your hands are too numerous to recount, but I do want to thank a few people by name — hoping that the many others who have contributed so much to my work will not feel slighted or take offense.

I'm grateful to Phil Hodges, whose insight and encouragement have helped me so much. I heartily recommend the *Lead Like Jesus* movement he co-founded with his colleague, Ken Blanchard, to anyone who enjoyed reading this book.

I'm grateful to Tom Nichols, who has taught me so much over the years and who will, I hope, continue teaching me in the years ahead. His enthusiasm about this work kept me on track when my energy waned.

I'm grateful, too, to Chuck Sauber, a remarkable octogenarian, entrepreneur and Christ-centered leader whose encouragement, wise counsel and example have enriched me so much in recent years.

I want to thank all my friends who don't seem to have the gift of faith — yet nevertheless strive to live good, honest, moral and ethical lives. You continue to challenge me and all my Christian brothers and sisters to live lives ever more consistent with the model embodied by our faith's founder — in the hope that one day you may be moved to join or return to the fold and help us do the work we were given to do.

I am thankful for the work of Wendy Tritt of Trittenhaus Design, who designed the cover of this book and handled typographic details. What is pleasing to the eye here is to her credit.

I am also grateful to all of my colleagues in various Christian communities who continue to inspire and challenge me. But I especially want to thank my associate Sue Sabrowski, who has the priceless gift of being able to redeem my manuscripts from so many errors while still encouraging me to proceed. She has made it a joy and a privilege to work with her for so many years, and I am especially grateful that she volunteered to scrutinize the first draft of this manuscript on her own time. I am grateful, too, to Dan McCullough, a friend and collaborator in many things, who performed yeoman proofing duty at the end.

Finally, I want to thank the members of my family who enrich my life in so many ways — by their example, their interest, their criticism, their questions, and most of all by their affection. Since my extended family now numbers nearly 100, I won't name them all. But I must mention by name my mother Joan, my wife Jane, and my children: Kristin, Erik, Shannon, Erin and Owen, as well as their spouses Nic, Robin and Shawn. You have made and kept my life purposeful, joyful, interesting — and lately blessed by grandchildren. I am especially grateful to Jane, my best and most faithful critic, who contributed to the development of this manuscript in so many vital ways from inception to publication.

All of you comprise the core of the vast conspiracy required to keep my life more or less on track. For that I am grateful to you — and to our God, from whom all good comes.

ABOUT THE AUTHOR

Dr. Owen Phelps, President/CEO of the Midwest
Leadership Institute, is a popular author, speaker, and mentor
who helps individuals and organizations achieve excellence.
His background includes experience as a business owner, an
executive in a large religious organization, and a member of
the faculty of Cardinal Stritch University's College of
Business. He is a consultant on the U.S. Conference of
Catholic Bishops' Communications Committee and a
member of the Catholic Communication Campaign
advisory board. Over the years he has served as a consultant
to faith-based organizations from Vermont to California. He
and his wife Jane live in Northern Illinois. They have five
grown children and six growing grandchildren.

"...While we have the opportunity, let us do good to all, but especially to those who belong to the family of the faith."

(GAL 6:10)

ARE YOU LOOKING FOR:
- encouragement?
- guidance?
- insight?

The call to Christian living is a call to leadership — and that call is universal. Jesus taught us how to lead. If you would like to know how to *Lead Like Jesus* at home, at work and in all your other life roles, stop by our website for a visit: **www.MidwestLeadershipInstitute.net**

REGISTER TO RECEIVE YOUR FREE MONTHLY E-DITION OF:

Synapse
The Journal of Organic Leadership

In *Synapse* we explore Servant Leadership and Steward Leadership. Sign up for your free monthly copy today: **www.MidwestLeadershipInstitute.net**

FIND OUT MORE ABOUT HOW:
- Religiously active people contribute more to the welfare of their civic communities
- Religiously active people lead healthier, happier lives.
- How Servant Leaders and Steward Leaders make themselves and their organizations more effective.

VISIT OUR WEBSITE TODAY:

www.MidwestLeadershipInstitute.net

To learn more about what it means to "lead like Jesus" and the *Lead Like Jesus Movement,* visit this website today: **www.LeadLikeJesus.com**

TO ARRANGE OR TO LEARN MORE ABOUT PROGRAMS BY DR. PHELPS:

Send email to:
ophelps@MidwestLeadershipInstitute.net

Send a letter to:
Owen Phelps, President/CEO
Midwest Leadership Institute
208 E. North St.
Durand, IL 61024

WHAT OTHERS SAY ABOUT DR. PHELPS:

*During my work with Dr. Phelps over the past ten years his insight
and targeted thinking have always impressed me. Owen knows
people, knows organizations and knows how to make both more
productive and effective.*

> – Greg Jiede, President/CEO
> Synergistic Networks

*Faced with the complexities of managing a small business in today's
rapidly changing environment, I have found the Midwest Leadership
Institute's ideas for developing leadership potential to be highly effective,
easily understood and able to be evaluated on an ongoing basis. The
methods suggested by MLI are the cornerstone of our Continuous
Improvement Program. The advice offered by Dr. Owen Phelps has
been invaluable to me both on a personal and professional level.*

> – Gregory Franchini, CEO
> Pierce Box & Paper
> Corporation

WHAT OTHERS SAY ABOUT DR. PHELPS:

I regard Owen Phelps as one of the most knowledgeable and most creative thinkers in the area of Catholic Church management and communications. His insights are always right "on the money."

> – Edward J. Murray, President/CEO
> National Interfaith Cable Coalition/
> Faith & Values Media New York, NY

Leadership requires a person to be task oriented, a people person, organizer, prudent, understanding, courageous, temperate and, to boot, charismatic. Come, see and conquer these qualities at Midwest Leadership Institute. I highly commend its mission of forming sturdy, wise and contemporary leaders.

> – Rev. Eugene F. Hemrick
> Director of the National Institute for the
> Renewal of the Priesthood
> Washington Theological Union,
> Washington, DC

I recently had the opportunity to attend a leadership seminar presented by Dr. Owen Phelps. The inspirational yet practical information, coupled with Dr. Phelps' honest, "down to earth" approach, held my attention from start to finish. In my professional life, I've often felt like an administrator who happened to be a Christian. Dr. Phelps reminded me that it's okay to be a Christian who happens to be an administrator. Truly effective leadership flows from the clear vision and direction that I receive through my faith. This seminar is a must for anyone yearning to put faith first in the nine-to-five world.

> – Karen S. Carlson, Administrator
> St. Elizabeth Catholic Community Center,
> Rockford, IL

Dr. Owen Phelps knows both how to lead effective organizations and how to nurture others to be effective leaders. He led our diocese's leadership through a mission and vision process that helped us to be more effective serving our diocesan church. I have solicited his wise counsel many times and always find his insights helpful.

> – Msgr. Thomas C. Brady
> Vicar General, Diocese of Rockford

WANT TO KNOW MORE ABOUT THE BENEFITS OF ATTENDING CHURCH?

You'll find it in the tiny, fun book *52 (Good) Reasons to Go to Church Besides the Obvious Ones.*

In just 62 small pages, author Paul McFate provides 52 good reasons drawn from scientific research showing correlations between participating in a faith community and having better, more satisfying lives and relationships.

There is a surprising amount of serious scientific research that indicates the more you participate in a faith-based organization, the more positive the effects will be.

Inspired to write this book to fulfill his spiritual duties as a godfather, McFate notes that "perhaps we all need a little support in the faith at some point or another."

McFate argues that going to church regularly can:
- lower your blood pressure
- increase your life expectancy
- strengthen your immune system
- improve your self-image
- improve your sex life
- create safer communities

Want to find out more?
Order 52 (Good) Reasons to Go to Church from ACTA Publications.
Just $5.95 plus shipping from:
    ACTA Publications
    5559 W. Howard Street
    Skokie, IL 60077

Web: www.actapublications.com
(Click on Spirituality, scroll down to Parenting)

Email: acta@actapublications.com

Phone: (800) 397-2282 in the U.S. or Canada